Goal: Finish before Dec. 2006!

WHAT TO DO
UNTIL
CHRIST
COMES

To my favorite niece,
Helene —
may God use this book to
strengthen your relationship
with Him — and help
you to get ready for the
biggest day in the future!
— 1 Peter 3
love,
uncle Dale

Hear what trusted Christian leaders are saying about this book ...

"Truth concerning the Lord's return was not revealed to satisfy curiosity or to generate excitement, but rather to produce godliness, and righteousness in the life of the one who is waiting for His coming. (1 John 3:1-3; Titus 2:12-14; 2 Peter 3:14). Every reference to His coming in the New Testament epistles is followed with an exhortation to such a purified life. While many have written concerning the truths of prophecy, few have applied it to daily life. It is this which the author does in this book. The practical applications of His coming are related to every phase of a believer's life, clearly, pointedly and forcefully. The book should not only be studied carefully but translated into living a godly life while we are awaiting His return. It deserves a wide hearing and application."

J. Dwight Pentecost, *Th.D.*
Distinguished Professor Emeritus of Bible Exposition,
Dallas Theological Seminary

"There's so much in the marketplace on prophecy and the end of the world, but so very little on "What To Do Until Christ Comes." From time to time you run across something that is so well-said that you wish you had written it yourself. This is how I feel about Dale Johnsen's approach to this vital subject of the second coming! He has packaged an abundance of sound, biblical content into a simple and useful format - WATCH, WITNESS, WORSHIP, WALK and WORK. Although his content is great, his passion that you "get it" is even greater! Don't miss this experience on "What To Do Until Christ Comes"!

Tim Timmons, *Pastor, New Community Church,*
Irvine, CA, motivational speaker for Success Seminars

"If you have difficulty eagerly anticipating your upcoming wedding to the Lord Jesus Christ, read this book and repent for having left your first love. If you have not been adequately preparing for the next earthly appearance of your great God and Savior, work through its applications. You will recover from your flirtatious spirit and contribute your part to the beauty of the Bride at the upcoming cosmic wedding."

Ramesh Richard, *Ph.D., Th.D.*
President, RREACH International,
Professor of Pastoral Ministries and World Missions,
Dallas Theological Seminary

WHAT TO DO
UNTIL
CHRIST
COMES

*Five Ways to Get Ready
for His Soon Return!*

Dr. Dale Johnsen

What To Do Until Christ Comes
Published by HolyGrace Publishing, Yakima, Washington
Copyright © 2000 by Dale Mark Johnsen

Library of Congress Cataloging-in-Publication Data
Johnsen, Dale Mark, 1955-
    What to do until Christ comes: / by Dale Johnsen
        p.   cm.
    Includes indexes.
    ISBN 0-615-11487-3 (paper)
    1. Christian Living 2. Prophecy
    Library of Congress Card Number: 00-103444

Cover design by Andrew McLaughlin, Copyright © 2000

Proofreading by Dr. J. Eric Halfhill, Mr. Laurie Stuck, Mr. Byron Wooten and Mr. Gordon Jaeger.

Printed in the United States of America.

This book is dedicated to Karen, my lifetime confidant, lover and best friend, and our two children, Peter and Beth, for patiently enduring extra days of work needed to polish and publish this manuscript.

This book is also dedicated to my earthly father, Edmund Merle Johnsen, who has been in our Heavenly Father's presence since October 26, 1993, giving me an extra reason to long for heaven.

Contents

Why Should You Read This Book?

Now that we have entered the third millennium, God's prophetic clock is ticking like a time bomb. Prophetic signs of Christ's soon return to earth are increasing in frequency and intensity around the globe:

Israel is reborn as a nation and Jerusalem has become the center focus of world attention.

Russia and Islamic nations are forming close alliances that threaten Israel's security.

World economies are uniting through global digital networking on the World Wide Web.

World governments are uniting under the European Union and the United Nations.

World religions are uniting to embrace the concept that there is no absolute truth.

Most books on futuristic themes tantalize your brain, but leave your spiritual life untouched. The practical issue of "what should I do?" as I wait for Christ's soon return is sadly neglected.

This book will fill that void by speaking biblical application directly to your heart.

This book focuses on the five commands from God's Word that directly apply to our Christian lives during these final days before Christ returns.

Those commands are summarized by these five W's:

Watch

    Witness

        Worship

            Walk

                Work

By understanding these five final commands, you can prepare for Christ's return with a healthy, holy sense of urgency, but without any weirdness or fanaticism. You will learn how to embrace a life of discipleship that will result in an abundance of eternal rewards in heaven.

This book is for you if:

*you expect Jesus Christ to return to earth very soon, and

*you want to clearly understand God's will for your life before Christ comes.

As you turn this page, ask God to prepare your heart to experience an intimate encounter with Him!

Introduction

Sixty-one percent of Americans believe in the second coming of Jesus Christ. Twenty-three percent of Christians in America expect the second coming of Christ to occur within their lifetime.[1] Do you expect to be part of the final generation that is alive when the Lord Jesus Christ physically returns to planet earth? If so, you'll want to be thoroughly ready for it in advance!

What do you expect? Now that the world's odometer has ticked over to 2-0-0-0, will we experience doom and gloom, or zoom and boom? Will this generation see gigantic tabloid-style catastrophes that wreck civilization, or an era of unparalleled peace, prosperity and optimism?

With either scenario, the truths in this book apply to your life in the same practical way.[2]

This book has one purpose. It explains to Christians the five most important issues that God wants you, the Bride of Christ, to focus on while you wait for your Bridegroom to come and take you home. It teaches you, in extremely practical terms, how to get ready for Christ's return.

Jesus says in Matthew 24:44, "So you also must <u>be ready</u>, because the Son of Man will come at an hour when

---

[1]David Briggs, "At the Millennium," Associated Press, October 26, 1997. An additional 14% say Christ will return within a century, and 26% more say it will happen within the next thousand years. This AP nationwide telephone poll of 1,016 adults was taken by ICR, July 11-15, 1997.

[2]Personally, I anticipate a pretribulational rapture. I believe that Jesus Christ will airlift His church from earth before hell's holocaust under earth's terrible tyrant begins. However, holding a different viewpoint will not diminish the applicational value of this book to you.

3

you do not expect him."

But, you ask, how?

2 Peter 3:11-12 asks this question plainly, "what kind of people ought you to be . . . as you look forward to the day of God?" For you as a Christian, God's specific answer to that question consists of five parts.

1. God wants you to **WATCH** until Christ comes. Matthew 24:42 says, "Therefore keep watch, because you do not know on what day your Lord will come." Mark 13:33,37 adds, "Be on guard! Be alert! You do not know when that time will come . . . What I say to you, I say to everyone: 'Watch!'" In 2 Timothy 4:8, Paul promises rewards in heaven for "all who have longed for his appearing." In Section One, you will learn how to **watch** for His return by longing for Christ's presence in the same way that a Jewish bride longs for her bridegroom to appear.

2. God wants you to **WITNESS** until Christ comes. Matthew 28:19-20 commands us to "go and make disciples of all nations . . . to the very end of the age." God's command to witness (Acts 1:8) remains in force until the entire world has heard the gospel. You must "snatch others from the fire and save them" from God's coming judgments (Jude 23). In Section Two, you will learn how to **witness** until Christ's return by "gossiping the gospel" because you love God, people and yourself.

3. God wants you to **WORSHIP** until Christ comes. Hebrews 10:25 instructs:

> Let us not give up meeting together, as some are in the habit of doing, but let us encourage one another — and all the more as you see the Day [of Christ's return] approaching.

Every time you celebrate the Lord's Supper, you hear the instructions to proclaim the Lord's death "until he comes" (1 Corinthians 11:26). In Section Three, you will learn how to **worship** Christ until He returns by serving in church, being Spirit-filled, and yielding to Christ's Lordship.

4. God wants you to **WALK** in obedience until Christ comes. 2 Peter 3:11,14 exhorts:

> You ought to live holy and godly lives as you look forward to the day of God. . . . So then, dear friends, since you are looking forward to this, make every effort to be found spotless, blameless and at peace with him.

In Section Four, you will learn how to **walk** until Christ comes by personally repenting of the seven common Christian sins that Christ uncovers in Revelation 2-3.

5. God wants you to **WORK** for Christ's kingdom until Christ comes. 2 Corinthians 5:10 teaches:

> we must all appear before the judgment seat of Christ, that each one may receive what is due him for the things done while in the body.

In Matthew 6:20, Jesus urges, "store up for yourselves treasures in heaven." In Philippians 3:14, Paul invites us to join with him, to "press on toward the goal to win the prize for which God has called me heavenward in Christ Jesus." In Section Five, you will learn how to **work** until Christ comes by using your time, treasure and talent in a way that will maximize your eternal rewards at the judgment seat of Christ.

We are racing to the edge of eternity. My heart races to think about seeing Jesus face to face. When Christ calls for His Church in the clouds, you will easily recognize me that day. I'll be the one screaming victory praises at the top of my resurrected lungs and grinning from ear to ear!

"Be on guard! Be alert! You do not
know when that time will come.
Therefore keep watch . . .
I say to everyone: 'Watch!'"

Section One

WATCH Until Christ Comes

A little girl had been listening in on a conversation that her mother and a friend were having about the any-moment return of Christ to the earth. At one point, the mother noticed that her daughter was missing, so she went to look for her. She found her upstairs, looking out a window. When asked what she was doing, the girl said, "Mommy, I heard you say that Jesus might come back today, so I washed myself and put on a clean dress, and I was hoping to be the first one to see Him when He comes!"

God wants you to have the attitude of that little girl. He wants you to also watch for and long for the appearing of the Lord Jesus Christ.

To "watch" for Him means that you live daily with the hopeful and eager anticipation that Christ could return at any moment. Jesus reminds us in Mark 13:32-37:

> No one knows about that day or hour, not even the angels in heaven . . . Be on guard! Be alert! You do not know when that time will come . . . Therefore keep watch . . . I say to everyone: 'Watch!'

Jesus tells us that while the specific date of His return cannot be predicted, the general era *can* be detected by watching the world stage being set for the tribulation through various signs.

Does Jesus really want you to be looking for these signs of birth pains? Yes! Absolutely! In Matthew 16:3, Jesus chides His disciples by saying, "You know how to interpret the appearance of the sky, but you cannot interpret the signs of the times." Jesus expected His people to recognize Him as the Messiah when He came the first time.[3] Likewise, He will hold you responsible to discern the signs of the times before He comes the second time. He wants you to observe current news events carefully in order to develop an ever-increasing hope for His imminent return.

The final curtain is about to fall on the theater of human history. God expects you to live with a deep sense of urgency, as though Christ may come for you today. He wants you to wake up each morning, thinking, "Perhaps it will be today!"

Christ's return is imminent. He is standing at the door of history. Can you almost hear that doorknob start to turn? Are you watching for the return of Christ with a high degree of eager expectancy?

If I could tell you with certainty that Jesus Christ is scheduled to "catch you up" to heaven tomorrow at 5 p.m., would you rejoice over it with excitement? Or would you start to groan about all the things you haven't yet had time to do on earth? Would you try to bargain with Christ and ask Him to wait until you can get married, or travel to Europe, or see your first grandchild? Or would you fling open your arms to Him without any hesitations at all?

Seriously, what would you do?

You've seen the comics that make fun of men with shaggy long hair wearing signboards shouting, "The end is near!" Just prior to the year 1000, men like this swarmed across Europe proclaiming an imminent apocalypse. Convinced that the planet would dissolve into ashes at

---

[3]In Luke 19:44, Jesus held His own generation responsible for anticipating that Old Testament prophecy would be fulfilled in a literal way. He points out that from Daniel 9:25-26, the Jewish leaders should have been alert to calculate the exact day of Messiah's entrance into Jerusalem. From the day that Cyrus issued the decree to rebuild Jerusalem (on Nisan 1, 445 B.C.) they should have counted out precisely 173,880 days (69 weeks of years x 7 x 360 days per year) to arrive at the Messiah's entrance into Jerusalem on March 30, A.D. 33. See Harold Hoehner's *Chronological Aspects of the Life of Christ* (Grand Rapids, MI: Zondervan Publishing House, 1977), 135-139.

midnight on the last day of 999, millions of people lived in extreme panic and sheer hysteria as church bells tolled the fateful hour.[4] Such behavior was as foolish as Y2K radicals hoarding huge stockpiles of weapons inside remote bomb shelters in Montana. Your God does not call you to give away all your possessions, cancel all plans for the future and sit on top of a mountain in a white robe to await the Lord. But neither does He want you to be naively living in "La La Land."

The time you have left on planet earth is running out, as rapidly as sand pouring through your fingers on the beach. Get ready to learn what God wants you to do about it while you still can.

---

[4]Jack Van Impe, *2001: On the Edge of Eternity* (Dallas, TX: Word Publishing, 1996), 14.

You are on your way to a wedding,
and that wedding is yours!

◆ *Chapter 1* ◆

God's Amazing Love

The moment the Lord calls you into His presence, instantly you will conquer your greatest enemy, the enemy of death. You will receive a glorious body that will never weaken or decay. You will begin to enjoy a wonderful new life that exceeds your wildest dreams.

Are you excited about the day when that change will occur?

A family from Appalachia, who had never seen life outside of the backwoods, decided that they would take a vacation to see what had changed in the world. So they drove to New York City. The mother stayed in the truck, while the father and his son walked into a large building.

At one end of the lobby, they stared in amazement at the elevator. The boy asked, "What's that, Pa?" The father said, "Son, I have never seen anything like this in all my life; I have no idea what happens in there."

They stood and watched in wide-eyed amazement as a very old woman in a wheel chair rolled into the small room. The doors closed behind her. They watched the lights go up and then down. When the doors opened again, a beautiful twenty-four year old woman stepped out.

The father looked at his son. With a twinkle in his eye, he whispered, "Go get your Ma!"

If you are a Christian, a time is coming soon when Jesus Christ will take your old wrinkled body in His "rapture⁵ elevator" going up (1 Thessalonians 4:16-18). By

---

⁵For a definition of the word rapture, see Appendix B.

the time He brings you back down to earth, you will be amazingly changed.

The best part about heaven is not that you will receive an immortal body. Nor is its most compelling attraction the streets of gold. It is that you will be with the Lord. Once Jesus Christ bursts through the door of history, your greatest privilege will be the opportunity to be with Him forever. Your eternal hope is not centered on an event or a place, but in a Person. Your most glorious privilege is that you will one day be married to your Creator, Savior and Lord.

A Cosmic Romance

Is it difficult for you to believe that Someone so big and distant and powerful as God really loves you as much as the Bible says He does? Is it troublesome to view yourself as a chief participant in a cosmic romance with God?

Think about this. The Milky Way, our galaxy of a hundred billion suns, is only a tiny speck within a speck of an almost endless universe. It was spoken into existence out of nothingness by the power of an infinite God. Does this fact make you feel utterly, microscopically insignificant? It should! Yet, God says that you, who are only a teeny-tiny human on a mere fleck-of-dust sized planet, are at the very center of His attention.

Professor David Needham at Multnomah Bible College gives an insightful illustration that helps you grasp the mystery of God's love for a microscopically faint fleck of dust like you.

God is a creator, a designer, an inventor, an engineer. With infinite knowledge and infinite power, He is the greatest of all scientists, the Supreme Scientist. Consider that role for Him as He pursues His experiments. Imagine He has created a vast science center, a sprawling complex covering thousands of square miles with laboratories stretching on and on beyond calculation.

Working throughout this Complex is a huge company of white-cloaked technicians, called angels, tireless servants of the Scientist who witness His limitless wisdom and creative power, and who move at the speed of thought to carry out His will. Every technician knows that the Prime Directive calls for absolute purity in the Complex. No hint of impurity, not even the slightest contamination, may be tolerated.

Within this Complex is a mystery so baffling, so deep, that not one among the numberless hosts of technicians can offer the slightest clue toward its answer, though they ache to know it. The mystery involves the Supreme Scientist Himself.

Day after day they watch the Scientist leave His other pursuits and walk toward one common-looking building, a single galaxy cluster out of all the millions of clusters He had made. In what seemed to be a strange obsession, He would always walk to exactly the same spot, into that one ordinary building, through the halls, past many doorways until, just past a door marked "ANDROMEDA," He would walk into the room designated "MILKY WAY." Inside this room were long rows of translucent cabinets filled with trays of billions of glass slides. Every day, without exception, the Scientist would walk down the aisles to one cabinet marked "ORION ARM." Then He would pull open one particular drawer. Finally, He would lift out one particular glass slide, the one with the tiny label, "Solar System."

He would take this common-looking slide over to His electron microscope and begin to move it around. He would see the sun within that slide, but move quickly past it. Jupiter and Saturn would come into view, but the Scientist would hurry past these as well, all the while boosting the magnification of His massive microscope, until a tiny bluish-green speck came into view. There he would stop, at a planet called Earth. He would spend hours looking at that one bit of blue-green on that one tiny slide. But why?

The Scientist told His technicians to pay attention to two infinitesimally small creatures on the face of that bluish-green speck, two thinking, moving, feeling creatures. "Watch carefully, My servants," He told them. "What happens with these creatures will be the final display of My creative capacity, the ultimate expression of My greatness." The Supreme Scientist informed them that by a process known only to Him, He had placed something of Himself in those beings. He had created them in His very image, something not even true of the technicians themselves.

The Scientist had developed a means of communicating with these creatures, of introducing thoughts from His infinite mind into the minuscule world of their own minds. He spoke in their language. They could hear His very voice. He loved these creatures on that one all-but-invisible speck very much.

Then, tragic news came. It fell over the Complex like a sudden shadow. An unspeakable tragedy had taken place. Something inconceivable, monstrous had occurred. Contamination had been discovered within the Supreme Scientist's domain.

There was no need of sirens or alarm bells. The Scientist's grief was so tangible it could be felt in every corner of the Complex. To make matters worse, the impurity had been discovered in that one building, in the one corridor, in the one room, on the one slide, on the tiny bluish-green speck. Some dreadful, incurable virus had somehow enveloped the two tiny creatures. As the creatures multiplied, the contamination multiplied, too. The whole population was dreadfully marked by some vile thing called "sin."

All the technicians knew what had to be done. The Scientist could not live with impurity. The speck had to be destroyed. He would have to take a bottle of sulfuric acid, draw out a microscopic portion, and let the droplet fall on the diseased speck. In just an instant it would fume and froth and boil, and that would be the end of it. It was unfortunate, but it was necessary. The Prime Directive demanded it. The very purity and integrity of the whole Complex was at stake.

Why, then, did the Scientist hesitate? The technicians felt a sense of foreboding, an inexplicable feeling that something, an incredible something, was about to happen.

The Scientist called His Son into the galaxy room of

the Milky Way. Together, they conceived a plan, a final solution to the contamination dilemma. Yes, the virus would be utterly destroyed. The cleansing wrath of the deadly sulfuric acid would certainly fall. But not in the way any technician could have ever imagined.

The plan would involve shrinking the Scientist's own dearly-loved Son down to the size of that diseased speck! No, more than that, down to the size of one of those infinitely tiny contaminated creatures on that speck. The concept was beyond comprehension. His own Son! His equal in power and wisdom and dignity. He would actually become one of these creatures, with the only exception being that the Scientist's Son would not be contaminated with sin.

The technicians were shocked with this drama unfolding on the microbe called Earth. They watched in amazement as the Scientist's Son willingly shrank down, down until he was lost from sight on the thin glass plate. There He lived among the diseased ones and ate their food. He shared their pain and cried their tears. After several years had passed, the day came when the Scientist drew His Son aside from the rest and caused all the ghastly filth and contamination of the whole planet to be absorbed into His body.

It would be called The Black Day forever. The Supreme Scientist drew out a measure of the white-hot acid and in great wrath dropped it on His own Son in order to kill the contamination of the entire race. The scream from the tiny slide could be heard in every corner of the Scientist's realm, "My God, My God! Why have You forsaken Me?" The Son burned, foamed, wrenched and died.

Shortly after this, the Supreme Scientist called once more on His awesome power and called His Son back from the far side of eternal destruction. The Father restored His Son to life, reinstating him in the Complex at His Father's side.

In the days that followed, from time to time the Scientist would reach down into that slide with infinitesimally small tweezers and pick up those human creatures who had responded to His love, those who were grateful to the Son for absorbing their filth and dying in their place. With deep joy He would lift them tenderly from the disease-damaged slide to a new, golden slide that was clean and fresh, where no sin, suffering, sorrow, or death could ever touch them again. Every time He would do so, it was a perfect exhibition of the awesome infinity of His love.

Did Almighty God send His own Son to suffer the very pangs of death and hell, unutterable torture, just so you could be transferred from one little glass slide onto another, far better one? Is the price Christ paid worthy of just transferring a bunch of creatures from a dirty place to a clean place, so we can skip around happily and strum harps forever? Is that all there is? No! There is much more.

Not only has He made us to be His sons and daughters, He has also made us to be joint-heirs to possess all that belongs to His Son. He is also in the process of preparing us to be His Son's eternal bride. The ultimate destiny for a Christian is to know complete personal intimacy with Jesus forever. In 2 Corinthians 11:2, Paul says – "I promised you to one husband, to Christ, so that I might present you as a pure virgin to him."

That is God's ultimate objective. God's Son came down to this infinitesimal speck in order to prepare you to be His bride![6]

It's true. If you are a Christian, you are the betrothed bride of Christ. You are on your way to a wedding, and that wedding is yours! The question is, what kind of wedding will it be?

Open the next chapter to find out!

---

[6]Adapted from David C. Needham, with Larry Libby, *Close To His Majesty* (Portland, OR: Multnomah Press, 1987), 101-113. Used by permission of the author.

◆ Chapter 2 ◆

Seven Stages of a Jewish Wedding

Many times, Jesus referred to the Jewish wedding as a way to teach truth about the relationship between Christ and His Church. Naturally, our tendency is to impose our own modern wedding customs and methods on the Scripture.

But when we do that, we miss the whole point.

In Western culture, the typical social pattern is that boy meets girl, they become friends, do some casual dating, then "go out," get engaged, perhaps "live together," and then marry. That is not the way it worked in the Bible. The boy did not pursue the girl he thought was prettiest. The girl did not flirt with and manipulate the emotions of the boy she wanted to nab for herself. The young couple did not "try each other on for size." No. Marriages came about by an arrangement made between the parents of the young man and the parents of the girl.

There were seven distinct steps that took place in every Jewish wedding. Each of these steps has a direct parallel to your marriage to Christ.[7] The more you understand them, the more your "watchful" excitement will grow when you think about Christ returning for you.

Step One Is Selecting

The father of the bridegroom took the initiative to decide when it was the right time for his son to marry. Then the father selected his son's bride. There was no flirting or dating involved. The father picked her out, and with

---

[7]Itinerant Bible teacher Jerry Benjamin provided these insights on the seven stages of a Jewish wedding.

approval from her father, arranged the marriage.

God the Father decided when His Son should marry and then selected His Bride. He then sent His Son to the Bride's house (earth) to win her affection, proving His unconditional love by dying for her. Galatians 4:4 declares, "When the time had fully come, God sent his Son," to the earth, to get His Bride (cf. Genesis 24). 1 John 4:14 says, "the Father has sent his Son to be the Savior of the world." God the Father selected us, the Church, to become the eternal wife of God the Son.

Step Two Is Purchasing

The bridegroom had to pay a bride-price to purchase his bride from her family. This bride-price was given by the bridegroom to the bride's parents.

The bride-price served two purposes. First, it functioned as financial compensation for the family's loss of the daughter's help in the home. Since she would no longer be in their home to clean, cook, tend flocks and work in the fields, her marriage brought an economic hardship to her own family. The bride-price compensated the family for their loss. Second, it proved the bridegroom's ability to provide financially for his bride. It showed he had the resourcefulness to acquire enough money to meet her physical needs. Because this bride-price[8] was paid by the groom to her parents, the bride was considered the groom's purchased possession.

Although this idea doesn't sound "politically correct" today, the clear teaching of the Bible is that we, the Church, the Bride of Christ, are Christ's purchased possession. In 1 Corinthians 6:19-20, Paul reminds the Church, "You are not your own; you were bought at a price." At what price

---

[8]This bride-price was different from the dowry, which was the money that the bride's parents gave to the couple as a savings account which would serve as the bride's "life insurance policy" in case her husband dies; in other words, the dowry is her retirement fund that keeps her from becoming destitute.

were we purchased? 1 Peter 1:18-19 tells us "that it was not with perishable things such as silver or gold that you were redeemed . . . but with the precious blood of Christ." Jesus purchased us on the cross. Our bride-price was the priceless gift of the death of our bridegroom for us. Jesus Christ died on the cross to shed His infinitely valuable blood to pay for the right to make us His Bride.

Step Three Is Betrothing

Once the bride-price was agreed on and paid, the marriage covenant was sealed by the drinking of grape juice or wine. The bride, upon approving of her groom, would drink the wine as the betrothal benediction is spoken. From that moment on, the couple was legally bound to one another and could not separate without a divorce (Matthew 1:19). [9]

When Jesus Christ met with His disciples at Passover the night before He died, He announced a "new covenant in His blood." With the drinking of wine, He sealed His betrothal to His Bride.

In 2 Corinthians 11:2, Paul articulates to the Church, "I promised you to one husband, to Christ, so that I might present you as a pure virgin to him."

Every time you take communion, it is a reminder that Jesus Christ is faithfully betrothed to you, for you have been bought and betrothed with the price of His blood.

Step Four Is Building

Soon after the betrothal covenant was made, the bridegroom returned to his father's house for about twelve months. During this time of waiting, he prepared living accommodations for his bride by building her a home.

---

[9] Normally, the consummation of the wedding was planned to take place approximately twelve months later. When the contract was finished, the couple was legally married though they were not to have sexual relations during the period of betrothal or engagement (usually one year).

Normally, this construction project involved his adding a new room to his father's house.

This is exactly what Jesus told His disciples as He was about to leave them in John 14:2-3:

> In my Father's house are many rooms; if it were not so, I would have told you. I am going there to prepare a place for you. And if I go and prepare a place for you, I will come back and take you to be with me that you also may be where I am.

Christ did not say He would come back and join His Bride so that they could be together where she is (on earth). He said that He would bring her to where He was, which is at His Father's house in heaven. (This is one reason why I expect the rapture to take us to heaven rather than immediately bring us back down to earth.)

During this building time when the home is being prepared, the bride's chief responsibility was to keep herself pure and set apart exclusively for her bridegroom until he comes to take her to the wedding at his father's house. Her days of waiting were spent learning how to please her husband. In the same way, during our time of waiting for Christ to return for us, our job is to become, as Ephesians 5:27 expresses it, "a radiant church, without stain or wrinkle or any other blemish, but holy and blameless."

Step Five Is Escorting

Once the dwelling place in the father's house was completed, the father of the groom again takes the initiative[10] to say to his son, "Now it is time to return to the bride's house and bring her back here for the wedding." When the bridegroom comes for his bride, he leaves the

---

[10]It was the father who determined the time of the wedding. When Jesus' disciples asked Him when He would return, what did He say? "No one knows about that day or hour, not even the angels in heaven, nor the Son, but only the Father" (Matthew 24:36). In Acts 1:7, Jesus said: "It is not for you to know the times or dates the Father has set by his own authority." This is because the Father sets the time.

father's house with two friends, the two witnesses required for a wedding.

As he approaches the bride's house, he announces his arrival with a shout. 1 Thessalonians 4:16-17 says,

> For the Lord himself will come down from heaven, with a loud command ['shout']," then we "will be caught up together . . . in the clouds to meet the Lord in the air.

When the bridegroom comes for his bride, he doesn't come all the way to her home. He stands outside and calls for her to come to him. In our case, the home we will leave is the earth. When we leave our home at the rapture, we'll meet Christ in the air to be escorted by Him back to His Father's house [heaven] where our wedding will take place.

Step Six Is Consummating

Once the bridegroom calls his bride out of her home, they return immediately to the bridegroom's father's house for the wedding. After a brief ceremony, her veil is lifted, and their commitments are sealed. Then they enter the bridal chamber where their marriage is sexually consummated with physical union. They are so consumed and preoccupied with each other that they stay inside their bridal chamber together uninterrupted for a long time, basking in the joy of their marital love.

This is the essence of the mystery of intimacy that Paul portrays in Ephesians 5:31-32 when he writes,

> 'For this reason a man will leave his father and mother and be united to his wife, and the two will become one flesh.' This is a profound mystery–but I am talking about Christ and the church.

Mutual sexual orgasm within marriage is the closest illustration on earth available to give us a taste of the ultimate ecstasy that we will enjoy forever in heaven with Christ.

Step Seven Is Feasting

As soon as the marriage has been consummated, the wedding supper begins at the home of the bridegroom's father.[11] Because the wedding is such an incredibly joyful event, all of the guests who have gathered will feast and party at the wedding reception for a full seven days of celebrative festivities.[12]

These seven days of the wedding supper of the Lamb represent the seven years of Daniel's seventieth week (Daniel 9:27). It suggests that our royal wedding, our wedding supper with Christ, and the Judgment Seat of Christ will all take place in heaven, in the Father's house, during the seven years of tribulation on the earth. We will be so obsessed and preoccupied with our union with Christ, being in His presence face to face, that we will not be concerned about all the judgments that are happening during these final seven years of trouble on the earth.

At this moment, every true Christian is intimately betrothed to Jesus Christ. We are promised to be married to Him with a definite, legally-binding covenant. This covenant cannot be broken because it has been signed with His own blood. At the rapture, Christ will call His Bride into the clouds and escort us back to His Father's house for the wedding and reception.[13] After those seven years are over, we will return with Christ to the earth.

Revelation 19:7-9 invites you to shriek with joy over that day:

---

[11] According to Matthew 22:1-4, the groom's father paid for the reception.

[12] When Jesus went to the wedding feast in Cana, He came on the third day of seven; this is why it was so embarrassing that the supply of wine had run out so soon.

[13] The Old Testament describes the Millennial Kingdom on earth as being a wedding feast, but this most likely refers to Israel's wedding feast, not the Church's. God the Father was "married" to Israel, and because of her repeated spiritual adultery, God divorced Israel. Through the judgments of the Tribulation, God will stop Israel's unfaithfulness, and He will re-marry Israel and establish with her an everlasting covenant. While God the Son is married to the Church, God the Father is married to Israel. Matthew 8:11 says: "many will come from the east and the west, and will take their places at the feast with Abraham, Isaac, and Jacob in the kingdom of heaven."

'Let us rejoice and be glad and give him glory! For the wedding of the Lamb has come, and his bride has made herself ready. Fine linen, bright and clean, was given her to wear.' (Fine linen stands for the righteous acts of the saints.) Then the angel said to me, 'Write: Blessed are those who are invited to the wedding supper of the Lamb!' And he added, 'These are the true words of God.'

You are on your way to a wedding! The Bride in this most spectacular, ultimate, cosmic-shaking wedding will be the Church. If you are a born-again believer, that includes you. On that awesome day, you'll be dressed in white, symbolizing the absolute purity of your spiritual virginity, showing that you have been made clean, whiter than snow, unstained by sin, washed in the blood of Christ, perfectly qualified to become the Bride of Christ.

Sometimes children will ask the question, "Why didn't Jesus ever marry?" The answer is, it's only a matter of timing. Jesus is betrothed to a beautiful Bride. His wedding day awaits the day of the rapture when He returns to receive His bride for the wedding (Ephesians 5:32; 2 Corinthians 11:2; Romans 7:4; Matthew 22:1-4).

At this moment, the carpenter from Nazareth is hammering together a house for you in heaven. He is building you a home, a mansion that is more beautiful than you can imagine, a place where you will live together forever. All the while He's building it, He is thinking of you. Don't worry; it won't be dumpy. He created this whole world in just six days. You can't begin to imagine what He can accomplish over 2,000 years.

The first time Jesus came to the earth, He came for His funeral. The second time Jesus comes, it is for His wedding. He's coming back to be with you. Jesus whispers, "I love you so much that I will take you back to heaven with Me so that we can be together forever!"

This glimpse of your destiny is so awesome, so mind-boggling, that it ought to infuse your daily living with wonder and praise. Knowing this should cause you to watch daily for your Bridegroom to come take you away. Your Bridegroom, Jesus Christ, is about to step back into history and bring you into the heavenly chapel so He can meet you at the end of the aisle!

God lets you know what He wants you to be doing while you are waiting for your Bridegroom to return for you in Ephesians 5:25-27:

> Christ loved the church and gave himself up for her to make her holy, cleansing her by the washing with water through the word, and to present her to himself as a radiant church, without stain or blemish, but holy and blameless.

Paul expands on this exhortation to holiness in Titus 2:11-14:

> For the grace of God that brings salvation has appeared to all men. It teaches us to say "No" to ungodliness and worldly passions, and to live self-controlled, upright and godly lives in this present age, while we wait for the blessed hope–the glorious appearing of our great God and Savior, Jesus Christ, who gave himself for us to redeem us from all wickedness and to purify for himself a people that are his very own, eager to do what is good.

As a believer and future bride, God calls you to be holy, blameless and pure. What part of your life ought to be cleaned up before your future husband comes to snatch you away? What blemishes are detracting from your radiant beauty? What area of personal purification that only you know about would be pleasing to your lover and Lord?

Before turning to Chapter 3, pause to pray. Tell Jesus you want to please Him. Go ahead. Take a minute to open up your heart to Him.

◆ Chapter 3 ◆

Longing for His Appearing

Does your heart pound with excitement as you anticipate that glorious day of union with Jesus Christ? God wants this wonderful expectation to motivate you to keep your heart, mind and body pure before Him as a spiritual virgin eagerly awaiting your wedding day.

At the end of Paul's life, the aged apostle wrote in 2 Timothy 4:8:

Now there is in store for me the crown of righteousness, which the Lord, the righteous Judge, will award to me on that day—and not only to me, but also to all who have longed for his appearing.

This special crown of righteousness waiting in heaven is reserved only for those Christians "who have longed for his appearing."

Do you truly long for His appearing?[14] There are two things that help to increase your longing for His appearing.

Signs

The first is signs. When you can identify multiple signs in society indicating that the rapture of the Church might happen soon, it awakens your desire to see your Savior's face. (You can review these signs in Chapter 4.) Although you must not attempt to set precise dates for the return of Christ (Matthew 24:36,42; Acts 1:6,7), God does expect you to be on the lookout for the rapture through discerning

---

[14]In the early church, Christians greeted one another with the word "Maranatha" which means "The Lord is coming soon!" Constantly they reminded each other about their blessed hope.

the signs of the times (Matthew 16:3; Luke 21:28; 1 Thessalonians 5:4).

Though you cannot predict the day or the hour, Christ has given you many clues that will help you to know the approximate era when He will return.

In Luke 21:29-30, Jesus said:

Look at the fig tree [Israel] and all the trees [other prophetic factors]. When they sprout leaves, you can see for yourselves and know that summer is near.

To "look at all the trees" you must stay aware of current events. You must commit to taking time each day to read the Bible and to read the newspaper, so that you will know what "each side" is doing.

In Luke 2:25, Simeon is honored as a righteous man because "he eagerly expected the Messiah to come and rescue Israel" (NLT).[15] God still honors similar eager expectations today.[16]

Trials

The second thing that will cause you to long for Christ's appearing is trials. Trials are a tool in God's hand to break your bonds with this world. When you hurt and suffer and struggle, this world begins to lose its glamour. You find out from experience that this world really isn't all that it's cracked up to be. That explains why Christians living in war-torn countries, starving to death, with no hope for tomorrow, are intensely longing for Christ to return soon.

God, in His sovereignty, permits pain for your good and for His glory. God uses trials to polish the purity of your

---

[15]*New Living Translation New Testament* (Wheaton, IL: Tyndale House Publishers, Inc., 1996).

[16]For instance, God expects you to try to figure out the meaning of the Babylon that will ride on the back of the Beast, because Revelation 18:4 commands you to come out of her. Revelation 13:18 invites you to calculate the meaning of 666, so you can see it coming down the road and stay out of its way.

life by conforming you to the character of Christ. God also uses trials to lead you to long for relief from the pain by yearning to be in the presence of your Lord.

When the load feels heavy, it's a clue that you are climbing. It is also a reminder to keep looking up in hopeful anticipation of Christ's any moment airlift to the top of life's mountain.

Ready or Not ...

Are you ready to meet Jesus Christ when He comes for you? Do you love the thought that He might come back for you at any moment? Do you long for the appearing of your glorious Bridegroom to carry you away? Do you really want it to be today?

I'm not asking you to be an optimist about it. An optimist is an 84 year-old man who marries a young lady and immediately starts looking for a larger house close to a school! I am simply asking you to be a realist. Jesus Christ really is coming back soon, and He asks you to be watching for Him when He comes. Will you do as He asks? Will you start watching for Christ's return?

Jesus commands you in Luke 21:28 to stay alert to watch all the signs falling into place: "When these things begin to take place, stand up and lift up your heads, because your redemption is drawing near." In Revelation 22:7, 22:12 and 22:20, Jesus repeatedly proclaims, "Behold, I am coming soon!" Revelation 22:20 invites us to keep praying that Christ will return soon by saying, "Come, Lord Jesus."

This prayer, "Come, Lord Jesus," is a prayer that God invites you to pray often. God wants you to keep on asking that Jesus Christ will soon return for His Bride. Why? Not because you want to get the "stuff" He will give you, but because you want to see Him in person, face to face.

All the indications on the world's stage are that we are living in the final scene of the last act. We are tottering at the very brink of eternity. The last curtain of history is about to fall. Until He comes, watch for Him. Keep one eye on the sky. He's coming back for you!

... Here He Comes!

You are privileged to be living in the most breathtaking moment in the history of the human race. You are poised at the threshold of eternity. You stand on a precipice overlooking the end of history. You are part of the terminal generation on planet earth. There may only be a few precious hours until the climax of history–Christ's return for His Church. For this, you should rejoice! Why? For perhaps even today you will see your Savior face to face.

Do you long for His appearing? Are you eager to go with Him at any time without notice? When you wake up in the morning, do you think, "Maybe I'll see Him today?"

If your answer is "No," perhaps you have overlooked the fact that you are a pilgrim and sojourner destined for a better land (1 Peter 2:11). Perhaps you have forgotten that your true citizenship is in heaven (Philippians 3:20). Perhaps you have become too comfortable on earth, too enamored with the world in all its pleasures, possessions and power. Perhaps you have falsely regarded earth to be your permanent home when it's really not.

If you cling too tightly to this world, it will keep your heart from hankering for heaven.

In the next chapter, you will uncover five sure signs of Christ's soon return that will open your eyes, quicken your pulse and motivate you to be yearning for His returning.

◆ Chapter 4 ◆

Five Signs of Christ's Return

Why should you expect Christ to return in your generation? Let's explore the five most significant specific signs that indicate that we are indeed rapidly racing toward the final era of human history.

1. National Israel Is Reborn

Israel is a very tiny nation, only half the size of San Bernadino County in California, or about the size of Rhode Island. Without the buffer of the West Bank territories, Israel is only nine miles wide at the center. Its six million people sit on the only land bridge connecting Asia, Africa and Europe. It is strategically stationed to have a major influence on the rest of the world.

The Jewish state of Israel is surrounded by twenty-two Islamic nations with two hundred million people (one hundred forty million of them Muslims). Together, these nations comprise a land area larger than the United States and five hundred times larger than Israel. Israel floats like a tiny island of democracy in the midst of a huge ocean of dictatorships and monarchies that are seething with anti-Jewish hostility and armed to the teeth. Despite its tiny size and population, Israel's influence is many times greater than all its Islamic neighbors put together.[17]

In Matthew 24:32-34, Jesus says that the leafing of the fig tree signals the generation when He returns to earth.

---

[17]Zola Levitt, "Israel: Earth's Lightening Rod," in *Foreshocks of the Antichrist*, ed. William T. James (Eugene, OR: Harvest House Publishers, 1997), 165.

What "fig tree" is He talking about? The Old Testament substantiates the fact that Jesus is using the "fig tree" to represent Israel. In Hosea 9:10, God states, "When I found Israel . . . it was like seeing the early fruit on the fig tree." In Jeremiah 24:1-10, God calls faithful Jews "good figs" while disobedient Jews are "bad figs." In Joel 1:7, God again refers to Israel as His fig tree. Jesus Himself uses the fig tree to symbolize Israel in Mark 11:12-21.

When the Romans leveled Jerusalem and destroyed the temple on August 5, A.D. 70, Israel's "fig leaves" withered. Israel, as a tree, was yanked out by its roots. Jesus tells you to watch for that tree, the tree of Israel, to be replanted. Then, when it re-blossoms and sprouts leaves on its branches, you will know that you are in the last generation. Christ says that the generation that is alive at this time will not all die before all the tribulation prophecies are fulfilled and He returns to earth.

The nation of Israel was reborn on May 14, 1948. That is when God's fig tree was replanted. Israel recaptured Jerusalem on June 7, 1967. That is when Israel grew its leaves: on 6/7/67.[18]

From an aerial view, from God's perspective, it appears as though Israel grew four leaves. Just before summer started in 1967, God's fig tree grew the leaves of the Sinai Peninsula to the south, the West Bank to the east, the Golan Heights to the north, and the Gaza Strip to the west.

Look closely at Matthew 24:32-34:

Now learn this lesson from the fig tree: As soon as its twigs get tender [at 19 years old] and its leaves come out [Sinai, West Bank, Golan Heights, Gaza Strip], you know that summer is near. Even so, when you see all these things, you know that it [Christ's return to earth] is near,

---

[18]In Luke 21:24, Jesus says — "Jerusalem will be trampled on by the Gentiles until the times of the Gentiles are fulfilled." It is possible that 6/7/67 marked the end of the times of the Gentiles. Curiously, the 6-7-6-7 sequence numerically pictures the age of man [6] being replaced by the age of God [7]; this 6-7 pattern is repeated twice, perhaps to assure us of its certainty.

right at the door. I tell you the truth, this generation [which is alive when the prophetic fig tree sprouts its leaves] will certainly not pass away until all these things have happened.

Which generation saw the fig tree sprout its leaves in 1967? It's the baby busters, Gen X'ers. THIS generation that has seen the re-budding of that fig tree is the terminal generation on planet earth, the most exciting generation in all of history.

Rapture Roulette

How long is a generation? Let's examine our options. Matthew 1:1-17 chronicles forty-two generations between Abraham (born 2135 B.C.) and Christ (born 5 B.C.). Simple division (2130/42) calculates a biblical generation to be about fifty-one years. Using this figure, Messiah could return anytime within fifty-one years (a biblical life-span generation) of 1967. This could indicate that Christ's return to earth may be as early as 2018, with the rapture on or before 2011.

However, others may argue that with human life-spans normally now extending to eighty years, the final generation should be calculated as eighty years. If you use this more conservative number, you arrive at the year 2047,[19] with the rapture on or before 2040.

No matter how long you calculate a generation to be, it is reasonable to assume Christ will return sometime before the present baby buster generation (which began in 1965) has died out.

Did you hear that? Jesus will likely return to earth in your lifetime! Though much maligned, Gen X will likely

---

[19]Hosea 5:14-6:2 predicts the scattering of Israel as well as her return to the land. Hosea 6:2 states: "After two days he will revive us; on the third day he will restore us, that we may live in his presence." In light of the 1000-year day (2 Peter 3:8), this may predict Christ's return 2000 years after A.D. 70, with the millennial kingdom fulfilling the third day. 2000 times 360-day prophetic years gives us 1971.2 years consisting of 365.26 days. From August 5, A.D. 70 (when the Temple was destroyed), 1971.2 years brings us to October 2041.

prove to be the most thrilling generation in all of human history to be alive!

2. Russia Is Allied with Islam

Ezekiel 38-39 details a prophecy about a future invasion of Israel from the far north (Ezekiel 38:15) by a land called "Magog." This invasion takes place "in future years" after the Jews have been brought "back to the land of Israel" (Ezekiel 37:12). Look at a globe; you will see that Moscow lies due north of Jerusalem. Russia is Magog.

The multi-national allies of the land of Magog listed in Ezekiel 38 are identified as the Islamic nations of Iran (Persia), Sudan and Ethiopia (Cush), Libya (Put), Ukraine (Gomer), Georgia (Meschech) and Turkey (Tubal and Togarmah). These nations have close alliances with Russia. Together, they will wage a bloody Islamic *Jihad* against the Jews that is designed to annihilate the "Zionist enemy," "liberate Jerusalem," and gain Russian control over Persian Gulf oil fields.

Watch the Bear

The mighty Russian bear that once threatened to devour the earth with an insatiable appetite for communist world domination is not dead. Since being forced to "release her cubs" in 1989, she has been wounded and weak, but her ability to create world havoc must not be underestimated.

Russia enters the 21st century with the largest nuclear submarine fleet in the world and 19,000 nuclear warheads. Poor ex-Soviet republics, desperate for cash, have likely sold many nukes to terrorists in Islamic nations. Eventually, thermonuclear anarchy will result in mass annihilation.

Marxist Russia once longed to dominate the world. The philosophical successors of that dream are Muslims who believe that Islam must eventually control the world. Islam is a dangerous false religion and a great threat to world peace because it justifies violence and deception to achieve its goals. Islam teaches the principle of *Takiya*, which says "fake peace when you are weak in order to wait for better timing to conquer your enemy when you are strong."

Islamic Iraq, led by renegade Saddam Hussein, refuses to play by conventional rules that forbid the production and use of biological weapons. Because these are much cheaper and easier to make than nuclear weapons, Iraq has stockpiled large quantities of chemical killing agents, known as "poor man's atomic bombs." These banned substances include anthrax, botulinum toxin and VX. When you keep in mind that Revelation 6:8 predicts that one fourth of the earth's population will die from plagues and pestilences, their eventual use is not just probable, but inevitable.

Islamic Iran, weary of living in the grim shadow of Israel's nuclear bombs, have signed a mutual defense pact with Russia. Iranian past-president Akbar Hashemi Rafsanjani says the goal is to unite all Islamic countries of the world in a coalition led by Syria (as the military leader) and Iran (as the spiritual leader). This emerging Damascus-Tehran alliance seeks to drive Western powers out of the Middle East and replace the Judeo-Christian world order with a new Islamic world order.

3. A Global Government is Emerging

The United Nations Commission on Global Governance has completed a three-year study on how to implement world government. William Knoke's book "Bold New World" states, "In the 21st century . . . a new spirit of global citizenship will evolve . . . and with it the ascendancy of global governance."

Former United Nations Under Secretary-General Robert Muller boldly supports the concept of a one-world government united with a one-world religion. He says world peace will ultimately depend "on divine and cosmic government" and an "alliance between all major religions and the U.N." He calls the U.N. "the body of Christ."

This movement towards world government is already in

full stride throughout Europe. A strong, united Europe has emerged from the ruins and rubble of World War II. The former Roman Empire is now unifying into the world's next great economic and political power.

The European Union (EU) came into existence in 1993. The Maastricht Treaty effectively united 345 million people under one European Union umbrella, marking the beginning of the end of national sovereignty. Like a glacier that cannot be stopped, borders and barriers are being erased.

Leader Hunger

Our world today lacks strong leadership that inspires vision and calms fears. We face a conspicuous leadership vacuum, as most nations are dissatisfied with the flaws and failings of their current leaders. We have lived without heroes, and we long for one. The stage is set for an impressive, superior politician to usher mankind into a one-world government. Soon, a new "rising star" leader with a charismatic personality will emerge in Europe to win the hearts of the world.

History is littered with speculations as to the identity of this man. The antichrist will have the oratorical skill of a John F. Kennedy, the inspirational aura of a Winston Churchill, the world-conquering vision of a Karl Marx, the bold determination of a Joseph Stalin, the military prowess of a Napoleon, the wit and charm of a Will Rogers, and the awesome genius of a King Solomon, all wrapped up in one person. Revelation 13:8 says, "All inhabitants of the earth will worship the beast." He will be someone who can be embraced by Muslims, apostate "Christians," New-Agers, Buddhists and Hindus alike.

Daniel 7 explains that this future world dictator will be recognizable by five characteristics. First, he will subdue three kings. Second, he will blaspheme God. Third, he will wage vicious war against the Jews. Fourth, he will toss out laws based on the Ten Commandments and try to change the dating of human events on the basis of B.C. and A.D. Fifth, he will persecute believers for three and a half years.

Daniel 2 accurately predicted four consecutive world empires: Babylon (head of gold), Medo-Persia (chest and arms of silver), Greece (belly and thighs of bronze), and Rome (legs of iron). It then predicts that a revived Roman Empire will rule the world when Christ returns (Daniel 2:41-45).

Daniel 2:42 describes earth's final empire as feet and toes that are "partly of baked clay and partly of iron." The ten toes of that statue are starting to wiggle (Revelation 17:12). Each "toe" is one of earth's ten future regional trading blocks. Aurelio Peccei, founder and president of the Club of Rome, openly advocates dividing the world into ten such regions of political and economic cohesion, eventually consolidating them into one world government. The Trilateral Commission and the Council on Foreign Relations also plan to break up the globe into ten regions (Revelation 17:12).

The World Trade Organization, World Bank and International Monetary Fund comprise the three legs of a well-orchestrated global plan to control the world's economy. He who controls all currency and economic trade will soon control the world.

All the technology that is needed to operate and control a global economy is already at hand.

4. A Global Economy is Emerging

Revelation 13:16-18 predicts a future time when a world dictator will control all global commerce by means of receiving a "mark,"[20] a universal economic code, that will be imprinted on or imbedded in a person's right hand or forehead:

---

[20]The "Multi-technology Automated Reader Card," or MARC, is a smart card now being issued by the Department of Defense to military personnel. It may be the prototype for a national ID card. Could this card foreshadow the "marc" of the beast?

He also forced everyone, small and great, rich and poor, free and slave, to receive a mark on his right hand or on his forehead, so that no one could buy or sell unless he had the mark, which is the name of the beast or the number of his name.

The mark of the beast will be imposed on everybody throughout the world, without exception. Without the mark, one cannot buy or sell anything. It will be the means to global economic control.

Prior to the computerized capacity to enable instantaneous global transfer of funds, the Bible's prediction of all buying and selling being controlled by the "mark of the beast" used to sound ludicrous. But because of recent advances in microprocessor technology, the capacity to manage a one-world economy is already here. Ours is the first generation in which the mark of the beast can be fulfilled literally by universally monitoring all financial transactions on the planet.

How? It will happen through the instantaneous networking of data over the Internet.

With our twenty-first century technological whiz-bang computer know-how, an economic monopoly controlled by a one-world dictatorship will be easy to implement. It is attractive, too. Cashless, electronic commerce would virtually eliminate most robberies, drug trafficking, tax evasion and counterfeiting. Plus, it's much cheaper. A paper transaction costs nearly a dollar, whereas an electronic transaction costs only three cents.

Smart Card Alert

Zebra-like linear bar codes, or UPC symbols (Universal Product Code), were first introduced in 1974. Then came magnetic strips that hold three tracks of data on your credit and debit cards. What's the next step? "Smart cards," a microcomputer chip embedded in plastic. Industry insiders predict that three to six billion people (most of the world's population) will carry some kind of smart card by 2007.

How can your positive personal identification be guaranteed? Biometrics is the answer. Any unique characteristic, such as voice, signature, facial image, fingerprint, hand geometry or iris pattern, can now be scanned into a computer in digital form and stored on a smart card.

Scientists can even retrieve foolproof DNA genetic profiles from a person's fingerprints.

However, electronic fingerprinting is less than 100% reliable, and experience shows that many people will emotionally resist using iris scans. These facts will force our society to adopt another ultimate technology that is utterly foolproof. It will be a biometric computer chip under the skin, quickly implanted by a hypodermic needle that can never be lost, stolen, forgotten or counterfeited. Imagine the convenience and security of electronically tagging all babies at birth so that all abducted children could be found. Alzheimer's patients, crashed pilots and lost hikers could be traced.

Microchip I.D.

Revelation 13:16 asserts that the beast will force everyone to "receive a mark on his right hand or on his forehead." The word "mark" [charagma in Greek] means "a mark or stamp that is engraved, scratched, etched, branded, cut or imprinted." The word "on" [epi] may be translated "on, in, or above." 1900 years ago, the Bible predicted a sub-dermal implant!

Injectable computer chips, with a passive radio frequency identification transponder, are already in use. Tiny glass tubes, smaller than a grain of rice, encapsulate the micro-circuitry. The microchip will be powered by a lithium battery that is recharged by the fluctuating temperature changes in the skin, either on the forehead or on the back of the hand.

Brave New World

Tim Willard, Executive Officer of the World Future Society, states the vision clearly,

> ...a number could be assigned at birth and go with a person throughout life. . . . Most likely the biochip would be implanted on the back of the hand so that it would be easy to scan. . . . At the checkout stand at a supermarket, you would simply pass your hand over a scanner and your bank account would automatically be debited.[21]

No fuss, no muss. It's techno-cool!

Revelation 13:18 says, "This calls for wisdom. If anyone has insight, let him calculate the number of the beast, for it is man's number. His number is 666."

What does 666 mean? It has three meanings: symbolic, numerological and technological.

First, 666 has a symbolical meaning. The number seven represents God, and the number six represents man. 666 is a human number that epitomizes mankind's collective rebellion against God, with each digit falling short of God's perfect number seven. Each six represents one person of the evil counterfeit trinity: Satan, the Beast and the False Prophet.[22]

Second, 666 has a numerological meaning. At the time this was written, the Roman Empire ruled the world and the Roman numeral system was used. Taking the first six Roman numerals of I, V, X, L, C, D, and adding them up, the numerical sum of those six numbers $1 + 5 + 10 + 50 + 100 + 500$ is exactly 666. This number represents a humanistic Roman world power. Six times six is thirty-six; if you add up all the numerals from one to thirty-six, they also total 666. Using the standard letter values used in

---

[21] Tim Willard, *The Mann Independent Journal,* April 2, 1989.

[22] Is it more than mere coincidence that 666 looks so much like $$$? Jesus Christ said that "money" is the chief rival deity for most of mankind (Matthew 6:24). Whatever a person loves the most will inevitably be worshiped as his god. Whatever embodies one's highest values will eventually become his religion.

numerical gematria, the Greek word "lateinos" meaning "Roman man," and the Hebrew word "romiti" meaning "Roman man," both add up to a total of 666.

Third, 666 also has a technological meaning. The line patterns on Universal Product Codes each represent a particular number. The two long skinny lines on the far left side represent a six. At the far right side, there is another six. Right in the middle are two more long skinny lines, another six. Surrounding nearly every UPC symbol there is a 6-6-6 already imprinted on anything you buy.

Check it out for yourself by studying your grocery store labels. All UPC codes already have a 666 secretly encoded by three sets of long thin lines. The one-world economy is close at hand.

5. A Global Religion is Emerging

The World Council of Churches was first assembled in 1948. Its ecumenical principles led to the mergers of several denominations, but it is not viewed as a powerful voice today. Another group that shares its "one world church" views is beginning to fill its vacuum.

In 1997, two hundred delegates from across the spiritual spectrum met at Stanford University to craft a charter to create a United Religions that stands parallel to the United Nations.

The United Religions Initiative states:

We, people of faith, called by our respective traditions to compassion, in response to the suffering of humanity and the crises which endanger our planet, wish to create a permanent forum where the world's religions and spiritual movements will gather daily to engage in prayerful dialogue to make peace among religions, leading to cooperative action for the sake of all. . . . All members of the United Religions do solemnly vow to use our combined resources only for nonviolent, compassionate action in our whole-hearted efforts to manifest divine love among all life on earth.[23]

Those who sign its charter agree to never proselytize people from other "faiths."

The United Religions movement is based on pagan monism, which teaches people to "look for the god within you" and focus on the environment, the economy and planetary peace.

Babylon the Great

According to Revelation 17:1-6, an ecumenical "world religion" will provide the propaganda support that the antichrist needs to consolidate his one world government. It describes the future one-world religion of Babylon as a great prostitute. Babylon is a code name for Rome.

After the rapture, when all true Christians are with Christ, the organizational structure of the Vatican will likely unite all unsaved Christendom from Protestant, Orthodox and Catholic churches.

I believe that in the wake of the shocking disappearance of millions of Christians in the rapture, a future evil Pope (false prophet) will embrace all Muslims as "brothers." Then, with the antichrist (beast), he will broker a final "land for peace" deal with the Islamic world that will permit the Jews to build their temple in Jerusalem. At the middle of the tribulation, the dominant Islamic faction will push the beast to follow the Koran's *Jihad* (holy war) strategy of conquering the world by eliminating the Jews first, then the Christians, wiping "the infidels" from the face of the earth (see Revelation 12).

In Islam, there can be no possible permanent peaceful equality with infidels.[24] The Koran's legal system requires that all non-Muslims must be converted, subjugated or

---

[23]http://www.united-religions.org/decla.html

[24]Michael Youssef, *America, Oil, & the Islamic Mind* (Grand Rapids, MI: Zondervan Publishing House, 1991), 44.

eliminated. Jews and new Christians will become martyrs of the tribulation, blood on the hands of Babylon the Great.

Are You Convinced?

You don't have to be a raving conspiracy nut to observe that the pieces of the prophetic puzzle are being put together with frightful accuracy at breakneck speed. All major props for the end-times scenario are already on stage, waiting for earth's final act to begin. Israel will soon be at war with Russia, Iran and Iraq. The prophesied global government, global economy, and global religion are almost here to help antichrist come to power. Christ's return to earth is very near!

When you see the downtown merchants begin decorating for Christmas, you know that Thanksgiving is near. In a similar way, when you see the signs of the second coming upon us, you know that the rapture of the church (which I feel is seven years earlier) must be close at hand.

You are living in the most fantastic era in all of history. From this day forward, you ought to be sitting on the edge of your seat every time you read a newspaper or watch a newscast on TV. Your heart ought to pump faster every time you think about the fact that your Lord could come in the clouds to take you home to be with Him, even today. You ought to be expecting to hear a heavenly trumpet blast any moment, calling you home.

Be on the lookout for Jesus Christ. Watch for Him! Your Bridegroom is coming back for you very soon!

This section concludes with the first of six Personal Applicational Reviews. Please take the time to fill it out, prayerfully. It will help the knowledge in your head to sink deeply into your heart.

◆ PERSONAL APPLICATIONAL REVIEW ◆

1. Honestly, how would you "grade" your personal attitude towards the idea that the rapture might occur today?

Excited beyond words?   Eagerly expectant?   Whatever, it's OK?

Somewhat hesitant?   I hope He waits until . . .?   Fearful and terrified?

2. For review, place the seven steps of a Jewish wedding in order:

Escorting Betrothing Selecting Feasting Purchasing Consummating Building

—————   —————   —————   —————   —————   —————   —————

3. What specific "blemish" in your life do you most want to clean up before your glorious Bridegroom comes to snatch you away?

——————————————————————————————————————

4. In particular, which sign in the world and which trial in your life makes you most long for Christ's appearing today?

Which sign?

——————————————————————————————————————

Which trial?

——————————————————————————————————————

5. In order to expand and unpack the simple prayer "Come, Lord Jesus," make this prayer your own:

Heavenly Father, I want you to be glorified through my life in these few short days before you return for Your Church. Ignite my life into a blazing torch for you. Burn from my life all the dross of mediocrity and apathy and casual Christianity. Give me the courage and self-discipline and confidence to live one hundred percent for you each day.

You have redeemed me, not to meander through my days with lazy living and stinkin' thinkin', but to be conformed to the character of Jesus Christ. Stir up in me a passionate desire to be deliberate and responsible and persevering about living the rest of my days for you. Wash away all the debris and dinginess of drab duty; purge me of my apathy and lethargy. Create within me a sense of urgency to start now to aim high for Your glory in my brief life on earth.

I offer myself as Your servant. I long for Your appearing. Take me, break me, and remake me to mirror Your will until I see You face to face. In Jesus' name, Amen.

Section Two

WITNESS Until Christ Comes

Many years ago, a Christian who owned an old-fashioned barber shop became convicted about his need to share Christ with others. So he determined that the next Saturday, he would share the gospel with someone who came into his shop. Throughout that fateful day, opportunities arose, but he froze up and found himself unable to say anything. By the end of the day, the tension was building, and he knew he had to say something.

Finally, the last customer came in the door and asked for a shave. The barber swallowed hard and said to himself, "This is the one!" So he cranked up his courage, lathered the man's face, pulled his straight razor out, and began to sharpen it on the leather strap.

As he walked around to the front of the chair, his voice was quivering and his hand that was holding the razor was shaking like crazy. He said, "Brother, are you prepared to die?" The guy immediately jumped out of his chair, smashed through the door, and ran screaming down the street!

Obviously, that method of sharing your faith is not very effective.

In light of the soon return of Christ, do you want to tell the people you know how they can be saved? Do you want God to use you as His tool to bring people to heaven?

No matter how nervous you are about it, God can help you overcome your fear and anxiety about witnessing. You can learn how to represent Him well without coming across harshly or judgmentally or argumentatively.

You can become an effective witness for Jesus Christ!

Christ wants you to prepare for His return by witnessing about Him to those who do not yet know Him. Until He comes, Christ expects you to be so passionately concerned for lost people that you will stretch yourself and sacrifice whatever it takes in order to share the gospel with others while there is yet time to rescue them from the coming wrath of God. Turn the page to find out how.

◆ Chapter 5 ◆

Gossip the Gospel

God has given every Christian this command: as you wait for Christ's return, witness for Him everywhere you go (Acts 1:8). God wants you to proclaim the good news about the forgiveness of sins that He offers to people in exchange for their repentant faith in God's grace (Luke 24:47).

The question is, when God opens up a door for you to explain your faith to someone who is not saved, will you be ready to witness for Him effectively?

1 Peter 3:15 outlines six practical essential ingredients to becoming an effective witness:

> But in your hearts set apart Christ as Lord. Always be prepared to give an answer to everyone who asks you to give the reason for the hope that you have. But do this with gentleness and respect.

This verse says that in order to communicate the gospel in a convincing way, you must be spiritual, knowledgeable, reasonable, personable, gentle and respectful.

Be Spiritual

First, you need to be spiritual. Verse 15a says, "in your hearts set apart Christ as Lord." You must make an inner commitment to Christ, setting Him apart as being the undisputed Lord over every area in your life. You need to trust the resurrected Christ to function as the absolute Lord of your universe, the sovereign God who is in charge of everything.

Is Christ the Lord over your family life? Is Christ the Lord over your financial life? Is Christ the Lord over your sexual life? Is Christ the Lord over your entertainment life?

45

To be an effective witness, you need to be genuinely spiritual. You must practice what you preach about the importance of trusting and obeying Christ as the Lord of your life.

Be Knowledgeable

Second, to be a convincing witness, you must be knowledgeable about the gospel. Verse 15b urges, "Always be prepared to give an answer to everyone who asks you." This means, be ready for impromptu interrogations. Be prepared to explain the gospel facts in an intelligent and coherent fashion so the person may make a decision based on the facts, not on an emotional appeal.

Colossians 4:5,6 amplifies this point by saying,

Be wise in the way you act toward outsiders; make the most of every opportunity. Let your conversation be always full of grace, seasoned with salt, so that you may know how to answer everyone.

Be Reasonable

Third, to be a convincing witness you must be reasonable. Verse 15c says you should be ready to give "the reason for the hope that you have." The word "reason" is a courtroom term for a public defendant who presents a logical explanation of the facts in a way that makes sense. It pictures a lawyer presenting his case to jurors in court. In the Greek, it is the word "apologia." Apologetics doesn't mean that you apologize for the gospel, nor does it mean you should pretend to be a hot-shot debate champ. Rather, it simply refers to putting into words what you believe so that others will be convinced of its truth. If a person asks you a question you've never thought of before, just say, "I don't know, but I'll try to find out for you by next week." That is reasonable.

Be Personal

Fourth, to be a convincing witness you must be personal. Verse 15d stresses that the answer you give is individualized: "to everyone who asks you to give the reason for the hope that you have." The use of the word "you" is very personal. It implies that you will be in contact with unchurched people who may be willing to listen to your personal testimony about your relationship with Christ because they know you.

You can't hide out all day in front of the television or computer screen and avoid contact with unbelievers if you expect to be able to win someone to the Lord. You need to rub shoulders with non-Christians. Then, when you do share the gospel, don't just rattle off a memorized canned spiel like a robot. Adapt your presentation to fit the needs of the individual. Be as personal as possible.

Be Gentle

Fifth, to be a convincing witness you must be gentle. Verse 15e reminds, "But do this with gentleness . . ." The word gentle or meek means that you don't get argumentative or loud. It means you don't hurt other people's feelings by being harsh or insensitive. It means that you will not twist arms or cram down throats or railroad people into an inescapable "decision" in which they cannot say "no." Rather, you keep in mind that it's the Holy Spirit's job to change their attitude and cause them to believe, not yours. Remembering this will help keep you gentle and kind.

Be Respectful

Sixth, to be a convincing witness you must be respectful. Verse 15f concludes, "But do this with . . . respect." The word respect, or fear, means "don't stomp on his human dignity" while you're trying to give a person the gospel. Don't barge in unceremoniously on his life and trample all over him in the name of evangelism. Be truthful, but don't be degrading. Be bold, but don't be brash. As Paul states in 2 Timothy 2:24-25:

And the Lord's servant must not quarrel; instead, he

must be kind to everyone, able to teach, not resentful. Those who oppose him he must gently instruct, in the hope that God will grant them repentance leading them to a knowledge of the truth.

To become an effective witness for Jesus Christ, you need to ask God to develop these six ingredients in your life.

The next chapter will focus on the tough issue of motivation. You may be honestly struggling with the issue of, "Why should I witness? The very thought of it makes me nervous. Why should I do something that feels so horribly uncomfortable for me?"

As you are about to see, the answer flows from Jesus' threefold exhortation to love in the greatest commandment: "'Love the Lord your God with all your heart' . . . And . . . 'Love your neighbor as yourself'" (Matthew 22:37-39).

Your motivation to witness for Christ will grow and flow from three sources:

*your love for God,

*your love for people, and

*your love for yourself.

As you turn the page, ask God to fill your heart with a powerful love for Him.

◆ Chapter 6 ◆

Love God: Obey His Commands

In Matthew 28:18, just before Jesus ascended into heaven, He proclaimed, "All authority in heaven and on earth has been given to me." Jesus Christ has the all-inclusive, unrestricted, universal sovereignty of God Almighty. This authority gives Him the official right to do whatever He pleases, with unlimited power.

What does He do with this unlimited universal authority? To what end does the all-wise God of Creation direct His sovereign power? He could have said anything, done anything, started anything. How did He choose to use that authority to accomplish His perfect will on earth?

The answer is found in Matthew 28:19-20a:

Therefore go and make disciples of all nations, baptizing them in the name of the Father and of the Son and of the Holy Spirit, and teaching them to obey everything I have commanded you.

This command is called the Great Commission.

The phrase "make disciples" is the only direct command in this verse. It is an emphatic imperative that stresses something that must be done immediately and continuously. This command is the centerpiece of Christ's marching orders for His Church today.

"Making disciples" is the heart of Christ's Great Commission for every believer. So, how do you "make disciples"?[25] By going, baptizing and teaching.

---

[25] By Christ's own definition, a disciple is an abiding, obedient, fruit-bearing believer who glorifies God (John 15:8,16), possesses joy (John 15:11), expresses love for fellow believers (John 15:9; John 14:21), and reproduces himself through evangelism (Matthew 9:36-38; John 8:31; 15:7-17; Luke 9:23-25; 14:25-35). He is a committed follower of Jesus Christ who can "teach others also" (2 Timothy 2:2).

Going

The "going" part speaks of evangelization, finding people who do not yet know Christ as Savior and introducing them to the gospel. The word "go" implies an aggressive attempt at outreach. It is not enough to simply sit back and wait for people to come to you. The extent of this outreach is to be worldwide, to all nations. No tribe, people group or language unit is to be neglected or ignored. All people need to hear about the grace and salvation that is offered by your Lord, so they can change from unbelief to belief, from doubt to faith, regarding who Jesus is and what He has done for them.

God may have not given a specific commission for you to "go overseas." Chances are, He has called you to stay at home in your own nation. But when someone from your church goes into a mission field, you are to "go with" him by making whatever sacrifices are necessary to support him in a team effort. God wants you to support missionary efforts around the globe with your financial support, prayer support, and by being open to go overseas yourself should God supply you with the desire and the open door.

"Going" includes the difficult task of traveling across the ocean, but it certainly also includes the easier task of traveling across the street, or walking down the office hall, or driving across town, in order to go to people in your own neighborhood. God wants you to extend the hand of friendship to them, loving them with the love of the Lord, so that you will earn the right to be heard as a credible, trustworthy person.

Do you resist being "a witness" because you think it requires door-to-door cold-turkey evangelism? Do you not see yourself as an aggressive "hot dog" in the elite corps of God's Green Berets, invading "enemy territory"? Are you not up for doing hand to hand combat with the devil?

Don't sweat it. "Going" doesn't have to be that scary. You can "go" by simply watching for the Holy Spirit to open up doors of opportunity for you to give a concise word of verbal testimony concerning your faith in Christ. Mention to someone how Christ has given you purpose, peace, joy and confidence in your own life. When your friend is open for more, share the simple plan of salvation. You can bring her with you to a special church service where she can hear the gospel message crisp and clear. You can also pray that she will place her trust in Christ and accept adoption into the family of God. That is included in what it means for you to "go."

Baptizing

But "going" doesn't end the process. To make a disciple, the second step is "baptizing."

Can you be saved and go to heaven without ever being baptized? Yes. God's gift of salvation is received purely by faith in God's grace in Christ and requires no "outer rituals" at all.

But, why in the world would you want to accept God's gift of eternal life and then not be willing to put on the uniform of the Christian by simply getting wet in front of witnesses?

Baptism in water is important. Although it is not a requirement for salvation, it is God's requirement for discipleship. If you have never been baptized, you may be a believer, but by biblical definition, you are not yet a disciple.

At first, baptism sounds like a quick, simple step that hardly needs to be mentioned. But when you consider how resistant some people are to taking this step after placing their faith in Christ, you can understand why the Scripture places such a high priority on it (Acts 2:41; 18:8; Romans 6:3-4).

Throughout the New Testament, baptism, the act of being immersed under water, is the meaningful, automatic first step of discipleship. It vividly pictures your identification with the death and resurrection of Christ. It is your primary outward mark of identification as a Christian. As a sign of your initiation into the Church, it publicly announces before witnesses your testimony of salvation. It seals your intention to live a new life that is pleasing to God. It was commanded by Christ (Matthew 28:19-20) and by the apostles (in Acts 10:48). It is the normal, expected response of every born-again believer soon after trusting in Christ (Colossians 2:12).

Baptism is like a wedding ring. Most married people wear one. If you don't wear this outer sign, many people will assume that you are not married. Likewise, in New Testament times, if a person had not been baptized, people would assume that he was not yet a believer.

When you are baptized, your immersion in water is a picture of two truths. One, it physically acts out what has happened invisibly, spiritually within you the moment you were saved. It pictures that you died to your old life and were raised to a new life in Christ. Secondly, baptism pictures what will eventually happen to you physically in the future when your body is literally raised from the dead to live in glory forever. It is an important second step in the process of making disciples.

Teaching

After going and baptizing, the third step involved in making disciples is "teaching them to obey everything I have commanded you."[26] This is the step where most churches tend to pour their greatest energy. It includes all forms of Bible education through preaching, Sunday

---

[26]What are the commands of Christ? A thorough examination of the imperatives spoken by Jesus reveals that throughout His ministry, He emphasized the following ten commands more than any others: 1. Repent from sin, believe in Christ and be saved. 2. Follow Christ in diligent discipleship. 3. Avoid false teaching and guard the truth. 4. Pray consistently, fervently and secretly. 5. Express love, humility and forgiveness in all relationships. 6. Use money strategically by generous giving to serve others. 7. Evangelize the lost by faithfully spreading the gospel. 8. Endure persecution from enemies with patience and joy. 9. Keep on watching for signs of Christ's return. 10. Stay encouraged; do not worry or be afraid.

School and home Bible studies. Specifically, God's goal is to teach you to obey everything that Christ commanded you to do and be, with no exceptions, nothing suppressed, nothing added and nothing watered down.

God expects you to trust and obey the entire inerrant Bible as the only authoritative guide for your personal life. Then He expects you to adopt the behaviors and attitudes that will shape you into a fully-devoted follower of Jesus Christ (Colossians 1:28).

Teaching involves your being trained and equipped with a working knowledge of the Bible and theology. It makes you a self-feeding Christian who can study the Word for yourself (2 Timothy 2:15). It shows you how to use the Word to fight off your enemy in spiritual warfare (2 Corinthians 10:3-5) as you detect counterfeit teachings and defend the truth (Jude 3). It leads you to discover your spiritual gift and find your ministry niche for serving God. It unleashes you and releases you to become a dynamic disciple who can disciple others as well as fill leadership roles within your church.

Christ's command was not to "make converts" or "make church members," but to "make disciples." Are you a true disciple? Are you a disciple-maker? How many disciples have you made? What are their names? Christ has called you to reproduce your spiritual life in others. Are you doing so? If not, are you spiritually sterile instead of reproductive?

The fruit of a disciple is another disciple. God wants you to bear much fruit (John 15:8).

Aware of His Presence

When you love God enough to obey His Great Commission, you are in for the thrill of your life, for then you can claim the comfort of the promise that Christ gives you in Matthew 28:20b, "And surely I am with you always, to the very end of the age."

In an objective sense, because Christ is omnipresent,

everywhere present at once throughout the universe, this statement is always true. The meaning of His messianic name Immanuel is "God with us." Christ will never leave you or forsake you. He is always right beside you.

Yet, in an experiential sense, the time when you are most aware of Christ's immediate presence with you is when you are obeying His commands. When you are conscientiously living out the three steps of His Great Commission, by being actively involved in the process of finding people, keeping people, and training people as disciples, you enjoy a much deeper and more abiding sense of the perpetual presence of Christ with you. Moment by moment, you are able to more fully practice the sense of His constant presence in your midst as you bask under His smile.

Nothing in all of life is more rewarding than that.

The authority to make a difference for eternity has been handed to you by your King. Christ's Great Commission, the marching mandate of the Church from now until the rapture, is to do all you can to get the gospel into the hearts of people you know.

Don't be like an arctic river—frozen over at the mouth. Don't shrink back from proclaiming that the hope of the world is found in a murdered Galilean. Boldly announce your allegiance to the crucified carpenter. Play your part in fulfilling God's global gospel goals.

God asks you to show that you truly love Him by obeying His command to witness to others about Christ. But He also gives you another incredibly strong reason to obey.

You'll find that reason uncovered on the next page.

◆ Chapter 7 ◆

Love People:
Rescue Them from Hell

A day is coming when the gentle Lamb of God who died for you will become the roaring Lion of God to execute judgment on all those who refuse to accept His offer of peace and reconciliation. Everyone alive is in one of two camps: those who are for Christ or those who are against Christ. There is no middle ground. Either one is in God's family, or out of it.

Ultimately, each person on earth will spend eternity either in heaven or in hell. If a person does not, by faith, choose to place himself under the blood of Christ by trusting in His death and resurrection, then Christ's substitutionary sacrifice on the cross will be of no benefit to him.

God's gracious invitation to heaven stands in stark contrast to the only other alternative there is, which is the lake of fire. Revelation 14:10-11 describes the final fate of an unbeliever:

> He will be tormented with burning sulfur in the presence of the holy angels and of the Lamb. And the smoke of their torment rises for ever and ever. There is no rest day or night.

Unending Agony

This sober, shocking passage teaches that the unsaved will suffer eternal punishment for their sins (see also Matthew 25:41; Jude 6-7; Revelation 20:10). The Bible teaches that those who refuse to put their faith and trust in the Lord Jesus Christ will endure God's wrath forever.

There is no annihilation. The unsaved will be "cast into the lake of fire" (Revelation 20:15) whose smoke of burning sulfur will forever rise as an indication of the endless, restless torment of those who are in hell.

Does the thought of hell trouble you? Unnerve you? Frighten you? It should. Hell is not a joke. It is not a myth, and it is not just a state of mind. Hell is an awful, but literal reality, a horribly haunting hard truth. You cannot sidestep it or ignore it. You must face its reality head-on.

When it comes to the subject of hell, one ounce of God's revelation is worth many tons of man's empty philosophical speculations. Unfortunately, some modern evangelicals are flirting with attempts to soften the orthodox doctrine of a conscious, eternal hell by teaching forms of conditional immortality or annihilationism. They use words like "extinction" and "extermination" to describe the ultimate fate of the unsaved. Their aim is to teach a "kinder, gentler damnation" that does not include the images of unending fire and pain.

However, in 2 Thessalonians 1:9, Paul declares that when Christ returns from heaven in blazing fire with His powerful angels, the unbelievers of this world "will be punished with everlasting destruction and shut out from the presence of the Lord and from the majesty of his power." The word "destruction" does not refer to annihilation or ceasing to exist, but to the ruination and worthlessness of a life that will be separated from the Lord forever in a terrifying pitch-black darkness where there is "no rest day or night" (Mark 9:42-48; Revelation 14:10-11).

Contrary to popular opinion, there is no companionship in hell. Hell is not a reform school where one gets purged from sin. There will be no "good times" to be found. Hell will consist of utter solitary confinement. Those who joke about wanting to go to hell so they can have reunion parties with drinking buddies are in for a rude awakening. Part of hell's torment will be its absolute, isolated, eternal loneliness, with no one to talk to and no hope of escape.

Eternal Is Eternal

In Matthew 25:46, Jesus compares "eternal life" with "eternal punishment." The adjective "eternal" in each phrase describes the same length of time. This word cannot refer to annihilation because someone cannot be punished eternally unless a person is there to feel that punishment. One cannot be "being punished eternally" if that person no longer exists.

Revelation 20:10 teaches that the devil, plus the beast and false prophet, "will be tormented day and night for ever and ever." The ultimate fate of the devil and these two most wicked human beings who have ever lived is one of eternal, conscious suffering. The phrase "for ever and ever" is literally "unto the ages of the ages." This is the most emphatic way of expressing endless duration possible in the Greek language. Other passages (Revelation 20:15; 19:20; 14:11; Matthew 25:41) show that the fate of the devil and his demons is the same as that of the ultimate fate of ordinary unsaved humans. Hell is a fate worse than mere death, a fate worse than annihilation. Jesus said regarding Judas in Matthew 26:24, "It would be better for him if he had not been born."

Hell is a place of sorrow, tears, anguish and horror, a place where one will feel the cravings of a heroin addict who cries out for a fix that will never come. Unbelievers will be absolutely alone and terribly afraid. There will be no pleasure, no hope, only pain, despair and total separation from God in blackest darkness and continually burning flames. Hell is a prison house of eternal damnation. It is a grotesque and hideous place of unending intense physical agony, a bottomless pit that lasts forever. Once in, there's no way out.[27]

---

[27]For a thorough theological refutation of universalism, salvation apart from Christ, and annhilationism, see Ramesh Richard's *The Population of Heaven* (Chicago, IL: Moody Press, 1994).

God's Loving Desire

God is eager to keep people out of that horrible place. 2 Peter 3:9 assures us that God is "not wanting anyone to perish, but everyone to come to repentance." 1 Timothy 2:3-4 reminds us that God "wants all men to be saved and to come to a knowledge of the truth." John 3:16 articulates it best: "For God so loved the world that he gave his one and only Son, that whoever believes in him [by trusting Him as your Savior] shall not perish [shall not go to hell] but have eternal life [in heaven]."

God wants everyone in heaven, but He won't force His love on anyone. He will not violate the freedom of man's will. He lets every person know intuitively that He exists (Romans 1:18-20; Psalm 19:1-6) and He writes His moral standards on each heart (Romans 2:14-15). He enables each person to see the doorway to salvation by convicting them of the truth of the gospel (John 16:7-11), and if a person wants to know God, He will provide them with more information (Jeremiah 29:13; Acts 17:27).

Every person who goes to hell has chosen to ignore or refuse these invitations from God. He has had the opportunity to go to heaven within his grasp, but chose to throw it away. People do not go to hell because Adam sinned, but because they refuse to accept the remedy that God has provided for Adam's sin. When people go to hell, they go there, literally, over the dead body of Jesus Christ who sacrificed Himself to keep them out.

God expects you to love people enough to try to help them avoid the terrifying, agonizing, eternal torment of darkness in the midst of fire. How? By amplifying through your words what they already know in their hearts to be true. It's your job to ask the people you know, "Why would you choose to spend an endless eternity in the rat hole of hell when an eternally glorious future in heaven is yours for the asking?"

God wants to use you to issue His merciful call to

repentance, warning people that they still have time to turn back from their sin and still escape the horror of eternal conscious punishment.

Do You Care?

If you really believed in the reality of hell, you should be willing to crawl on your hands and knees over hot coals or over beds of nails in order to keep just one other person from ever going there. You should be willing to give up a few luxuries and comforts on earth in order to better financially support the spread of the gospel throughout your community and world. You should be willing to dedicate yourself completely to doing whatever the Lord asks you to do obediently, including being a missionary anywhere God needs you the most.

You should certainly be eager to do little simple things, such as inviting a few friends to church and by extending a more-than-superficial friendship to guests at your church.

How passionately do you care about the lost people around you? Are you willing to give up a couple nights of television in order to build a relationship with an unsaved neighbor or friend? Are you willing to invite your friend to be your guest at your church next Sunday morning?

(If you are afraid your church service would scare him away, find another church that won't.)

Paul's passionate love for people leads him to write in Romans 9:2, 10:1, "I have great sorrow and unceasing anguish in my heart" for "my heart's desire and prayer to God for the Israelites is that they may be saved."

As you think about your relatives and friends burning forever in hell, are you moved to sorrow and anguish in your heart? Do you earnestly long to see them be saved?

Do you truly love people enough to tell them how they can escape hell through placing their trust in Jesus Christ? The next chapter will give you one more reason to do something about it.

Your Coach, Jesus Christ, is
calling you to dust off your
running shoes, stand up, move away
from the sidelines and begin to
take laps around His track.

• Chapter 8 •

Love Yourself:

Pursue Eternal Rewards

When you make the inner commitment to look for open doors to insert a word for God into your conversations, God will honor you in eternity. He will cause your life to shine like a star. Daniel 12:3 promises, "Those who are wise will shine like the brightness of the heavens, and those who lead many to righteousness, like the stars for ever and ever."

In Philippians 2:15-16, God says He wants you to be "blameless and pure, children of God without fault in a crooked and depraved generation, in which you shine like stars in the universe as you hold out the word of life." If you want to become a "star" in God's eyes, you will be "wise" by seeking to "lead many to righteousness" by witnessing to people, gossiping the gospel, leading others to a saving knowledge of Jesus Christ.

On earth, you may never stand under the spotlight and receive the applause of people, but if you are faithful as a witness, God will make you a "star Christian" forever.

Run the Race

The Apostle Paul motivates you to run the race of winning people to faith in Christ by assuming the role of a coach who is giving a locker room challenge to his well-disciplined athletes. He writes in 1 Corinthians 9:24-25:

Do you not know that in a race all the runners run, but only one gets the prize? Run in such a way as to get the prize. Everyone who competes in the games goes into strict training. They do it to get a crown that will not last;

but we do it to get a crown that will last forever.

These verses drip with the sweat of "jocks." You can almost hear their grunts and groans as you read the text. God wants you to know that you are in a "race." He wants you to understand the award system at the finish line. The Judge of this event wants you to know how He keeps score so that you will know how to win the race and receive the prize.

The prize Paul talks about here is not salvation. Salvation is not a prize that you win by effort; it is a gift that you receive by faith. But as soon as you are saved, you are thrust into a race, a race toward the goal of bringing as many people as possible to faith in Christ through evangelism. The winners of this race will receive the prize of eternal rewards from God.

Athletes would come from every part of the Mediterranean area to compete in the biennial Isthmian Games that were held in a stadium ten miles outside of Corinth. There, world-class athletes competed in foot races, broad jumping, discus throwing, javelin hurling, wrestling, boxing and gymnastics. Before competing, each athlete was required to take an oath affirming that he had followed a strict diet and training regimen for the previous ten months. He had to have sacrificed certain indulgences and delightful foods.

It was the price he had to pay for the privilege of striving for the winner's crown.

In 1 Corinthians 9:25, the word "compete" in the Greek is the word *agonizomai*. It means just what it sounds like: to agonize, to strain your strength to your limit of endurance. The phrase "self-control" or "strict training" literally means to have the "strength within" to gain mastery over your appetites and passions rather than giving in to impulse or overindulgence.

What a rebuke to our half-hearted, flabby hesitancy to witness simply because it is "not convenient" or "not comfortable" for us to do it!

Do you tend to pamper yourself with thinking that it is "good enough" to be a "silent witness"? That approach is soft, easy and lazy. It avoids the rigorous discipline of intense prayer, dedicated study and memorization of Scripture. It avoids the aggressive pursuit of close relationships with non-Christians. It is a cop-out. When you hide yourself within a safe Christian subculture, as a fortress to protect you from the harshness of interacting too much with the real world, it is a sin. It disregards God's command that you witness to lost people, out loud.

Training Required

As a Christian, God instructs you to be in strict training for this race. God wants you to be bold and intentional about keeping your spiritual life in top shape so that you will befriend non-Christians, show them God's love, lead them to faith in Christ and disciple them to spiritual growth.

Why? Because for doing that, God promises you a special reward that will last forever.

The winner of each event in the Isthmian games received not a gold medal draped around their neck, but rather, a leafy crown, a pine wreath placed upon their head. Even to this day, the NCAA emblem is a picture of a boy being given a pine wreath. The winners also received other rewards, such as a lifetime exemption from taxes, a tuition-free education and statues of themselves alongside the road that led to the game site. But the most prestigious part of their reward was the pine wreath.

These young men would work diligently for ten months, making many personal sacrifices to whip their bodies and minds into shape for the purpose of winning the privilege to wear a crown that wilts and fades away. By contrast, when you make personal sacrifices in order to win other people to Christ and serve Him, God offers you a crown that will never fade away.

God holds out to you the incentive of rewards that

endure for eternity.

The best news is that in God's race of witnessing, not just one person wins. God's winning prize will go not just to the one individual in history who has won the most people to Christ in his lifetime, such as Bill Bright, Billy Graham or D.L. Moody. Instead, God challenges every believer to "Run to win!" Run as if you are in heavy competition, as if you might lose if you don't press on with your best effort. Run in such a way that you can visualize your heaving chest breaking the tape at the finish line. Be like a marathon runner who is in this race for the duration.

Why? Because if you run this race wholeheartedly, giving it your best effort, you will win an eternal prize.

Meet Your Competition

You are not competing against other Christians in this race. You are competing only against the weaknesses of your own flesh. No one can run your race for you and you can't blame others if you fail to win. But by the enabling power of the Holy Spirit, you have the potential to win.

Not every Christian will win this race. Victory is not automatic. Some will choose to lose. Some Christians will not press toward the goal of winning the prize of God's reward. Some will choose to live carelessly and selfishly. They will end up feeling ashamed to meet Christ when He returns.

Whether you will be a winner or a loser in this race is entirely up to you.

What makes the difference? It is not that some are genetically predisposed to witnessing while others are not. It is not that those who were born into Christian families have an unfair advantage over those who were not. It is not that those who have a splashy, sensational testimony about how they were delivered from the gutter of immorality, drugs and rebellion receive more points than those who were being force-fed memory verses at the age of three. No. There are simply no excuses to be made. God is perfectly fair to evaluate you based on your own unique situation.

You are not racing against any other person at all. You are racing only against you. If you don't win your race, you will have no one to blame but yourself.

To win this prize, you don't need the gift of evangelism. You don't need to go knocking on doors or handing out tracts at the Mall. You don't even need to complete an Evangelism Explosion course before you start. But you do need to be willing to be socially adaptable, to become all things to all men so that by all possible means, through building up your friendships with unbelievers, your witness might be used of God to save some (1 Corinthians 9:22-23).

Unlike the runners in Corinth who knew how long their race would be, you don't know when your race will end. You may have twenty years left, or you may not have until the end of the day before God calls you home. That's why you need to be diligent in the time you have left to do your very best. Make each day count for Christ as if it may be your last.

Purposeful Punches

In 1 Corinthians 9:26, Paul comments that in light of the uncertainty of how much time he has left, "I do not run like a man running aimlessly; I do not fight like a man beating the air." Paul always kept his ultimate goal in mind, seeking to win as many people to Christ in his lifetime as possible. He did not run this race with uncertainty, haphazardly or aimlessly, but with a clear purpose, with his eyes glued to the tape.

Do you?

Paul switches his analogy to boxing: "I do not fight like a man beating the air." He is not wildly swinging meaningless punches that miss the opponent and merely fan the air. He's not just shadow boxing. Rather, when he cocks his fist back to swing, he makes sure he lands squarely on his target. He runs with purpose and he hits with purpose.

His purpose is to win as many people to Christ as possible in his lifetime.

Have you ever adopted that purpose for your own life? You don't have to be an apostle, an evangelist or a pastor to adopt that goal. You just need to be you, living out your Christian faith in the world in a purposeful, focused way. You must choose to be mindful of your potential impact on the lives of non-Christians, always thinking about how God can use your love, your life and your words to bring somebody new into the kingdom of God.

That sounds like a lot of effort! How does Paul get himself into shape for such a strenuous, focused life? 1 Corinthians 9:27 states, "I beat my body and make it my slave." This word "beat" or "discipline" means literally to "bruise with a blow" or "to strike under the eye." In first century boxing, this was the technical term for a "knock out." Paul knocks himself out, even to the point of giving his own flesh a black eye, in order to make sure that his flesh doesn't get in the way of achieving his all-important life goal.

Paul is not advocating physical self-mutilation, but spiritual self-restraint and the exercise of full self-control over his soul. He lives a thoroughly disciplined Christian life for the sake of the gospel. He challenges you to be diligent to deepen your walk with God in prayer, to feed your soul with God's Word, to stay away from sin. He rebukes the half-hearted, out-of-shape laziness that results in doing almost nothing to give the gospel to lost people who are headed for hell.

Paul looks at Christians who think it's a big chore just to get up on Sunday morning to go to church once a week, and says, "If you get winded doing that, you're way out of shape. You need some spiritual exercise to whip yourself back into healthy condition."

Don't Disqualify

In order to subdue your body and make it your slave, you must learn to say "No" to proud selfism, lustful sensualism and overindulgent materialism. You must refuse to pamper your flesh with sin. You must discipline and train yourself to be godly (1 Timothy 4:7).

At the end of 1 Corinthians 9:27, Paul voices concern about the possibility of his being "disqualified for the prize." The King James says, "lest I be a castaway." This verse has led many people to conclude that the Apostle Paul thought he could lose his eternal salvation.

That is not what he is talking about at all. This race he is talking about is not a race for his own salvation. It is a race for the salvation of others.

Paul does not want to be disqualified from the gospel ministry because of sin in his life. He doesn't want to lose any opportunities to lead people to Christ as a result of him ruining his testimony for Christ. He does not want God to have to discipline him for misbehavior by taking him off of the front lines and putting his ministry on the shelf.

To be disqualified means you have lost the opportunity to be an effective witness to others. It means that you have lost the right to be heard, that you have destroyed your testimony so thoroughly that unsaved people no longer take you seriously when you talk about spiritual things.

It also means you have forfeited some of your eternal rewards at the judgment seat of Christ.

You can be disqualified by not disciplining your body with regards to sexual immorality, drug abuse or drunkenness; by not disciplining your tongue with respect to bitter gossip and harsh, hurtful words; or by not disciplining your stewardship of your money through dishonesty or greed.

You also effectively disqualify yourself from being an effective witness by wasting too much time on non-essential things, by not limiting the time you spend sitting in front of the great hour devourer, the TV, or by being excessively devoted to web surfing or sports watching. In other words, do not let the "good" things in your life subtly keep you away from the "best" thing, which is the race to win souls for the kingdom of God.

Win the Prize!

Do you want your life to count, to make a difference for eternity? Do you want to strive for eternal rewards? Then make a decision to not live for things that will, in the end, amount to nothing. Give up the incessant pursuit of stuff that will one day wither and crumble into dust. Decide that you will invest your life in what lasts forever. Make it a top priority in your life to do whatever you can, by all possible means, to save some. Pay the price to stay spiritually available to run the race as a credible witness so that you will never become "disqualified."

Eugene Peterson's paraphrase of the New Testament in *The Message* renders 1 Corinthians 9:26 this way:

I don't know about you, but I'm running hard for the finish line. I'm giving it everything I've got. No sloppy living for me! I'm staying alert and in top condition. I'm not going to be caught napping.[28]

How is it in your life? Can you say that you are in active training, right now, for the witnesses' race? Is your body the slave of your spirit? Are you living each day with the purpose of making yourself adaptable and available to lead other people toward Christ?

Is the smell of victory in the air? Or, have you already dropped out of the race?

Have you already collapsed somewhere off the side of the track, complaining that it's just too hard to keep going any longer for the Lord? Have you given up on the hope that you could ever win that crown, thinking that the Lord

---

[28]Eugene Peterson, *The Message* (Colorado Springs, CO: NavPress, 1993).

could never use you to bring somebody to heaven? Have you temporarily disqualified yourself from even having the right to share the gospel with others by allowing and harboring sin in your life that should not be there?

This is your life. This is your race. Do you really care if you win?

Do not be a Christian who nonchalantly stands around on God's racetrack as if the prize will be won automatically without any running at all. Do not daydream, loiter and fold your arms as you slowly walk along the track, stopping to look at all the pretty distractions along the way. If you do that, you won't make it to the finish line because you've forgotten the most important reason why God has left you here on earth: to proclaim God's way of salvation to people who are lost.

If you want to win this race, you have to run the race. You need to witness to other people about Christ. There is a real prize out there worth running for. To run the race, you must be willing to get close to people who need the Lord. You must practice social self-denial, so you do not offend those you want to witness to. You must practice spiritual self-discipline, even when it hurts.[29]

What sacrifices are you willing to make in order to receive an eternal gold medal from God? What pain are you willing to endure? Your Coach, Jesus Christ, is calling you to dust off your running shoes, stand up, move away from the sidelines and begin to take laps around His track.

You, as a "lay person," make the most effective witness, because you are already strategically located to

---

[29]In the 1976 Summer Olympics, twenty-six year old Shun Fujimoto competed in team gymnastics for Japan. In his quest for the gold medal, Fujimoto suffered a broken right knee in the floor exercise. But his physical ailment did not stop him. During the next week, he still competed in his strongest event, the rings. His routine was excellent. What really astounded everyone was that he squarely dismounted with a triple somersault twist on a broken right knee. When asked concerning this feat, he said, "Yes, the pain shot through me like a knife. It brought tears to my eyes. But now I have a gold medal and the pain is gone."

witness to those in your world. God has already planted you as His missionary in your neighborhood and in your own vocational village. People are watching your life, and when you witness for Christ, people know it's authentic, from your heart.

Go for Gold

If you are not yet involved in the process of verbally sharing the gospel, you are not yet running your race. Get off the bench. Go for the gold. Push to the finish for the glory of Christ.

The fact is, you live on a mission field. People all around you are hurting, desperately longing for someone to love them and understand them and feel their pain. You live in a post-Christian, postmodern culture. The influence of Christianity in society has decayed and deteriorated at the same time that secularism, materialism and relativism have strongly advanced.

In that setting, God has given you a job to do for Him.

Your job is to populate heaven with as many people as you possibly can. You do that by inviting people to open the door of their lives to receive Christ as Savior.

When you do that (which is life's most unselfish deed), you are not only loving God and loving others; you also are loving yourself. What a way to live!

But let's not duck the reality that sometimes, those who live that way pay a big price. Are you willing to take that risk? Are you a "spiritual Marine"?

To honestly consider the cost of doing so, read on.

◆ *Chapter 9* ◆

The Peril of Persecution

Are you afraid of the thought of witnessing? Do you feel like the cost of obedience might be too painful? I won't minimize the truth or lie to you. The fact is, when you witness for Christ, you could possibly suffer for Christ. But if and when that happens, you don't need to be intimidated by it. You shouldn't be terrified or traumatized by it to the point that you would cringe and cower and run away. Instead, God calls you to be confident. He wants you to remember that it is a high privilege to be able to suffer unjust persecution for Christ. Jesus says in Matthew 5:10-12:

> Blessed are those who are persecuted because of righteousness, for theirs is the kingdom of heaven. Blessed are you when people insult you, persecute you and falsely say all kinds of evil against you because of me. Rejoice and be glad, because great is your reward in heaven, for in the same way they persecuted the prophets who were before you.

Jesus teaches that when you have the experience of being persecuted for your faith,[30] you enter an elite class of saints. That is why, in Acts 5:41, the apostles rejoiced that "they had been counted worthy of suffering disgrace" for the name of Christ.

The same principle is still true today. When you are hassled and harangued for your faith, God wants you to rejoice over it as a blessing. If you are picked on for being a Christian, God wants you to regard this as evidence that

---

[30]It's not persecution if problems come because you have been rude and obnoxious and pushy!

you are very special in God's sight.

If you can maintain that kind of confident attitude as a Christian, you'll never fall for the cheap tactics of those shallow critics who try to intimidate you into silence by confronting you about your faith. It won't disturb you or shake you up or cause you to panic when somebody unleashes some pent-up verbal displeasure on you all because he doesn't like you telling him about heaven.

As a Christian, your job is simple. It is to invite people to come to Jesus Christ by grace, through faith alone. You are to echo Christ's words in Revelation 22:17, saying, "Whoever is thirsty, let him come; and whoever wishes, let him take the free gift of the water of life."

A Simple Invitation

The gospel is so simple that its very simplicity can be a stumbling block to people believing it. Most people feel they need to "do" something to earn their salvation, even though God insists it is a free gift. People think they have to work for it, while God says all they have to do is to "come."

Your job is to show people how simple salvation really is. Jesus tells us that it is as simple as drinking water (John 4:14, John 7:37-38), as simple as eating bread (John 6:35,51) and as simple as walking through a door (John 10:9a). Paul says it is as simple as receiving a gift (Romans 6:23), as simple as believing that Jesus Christ is Lord (Romans 10:9) and as simple as calling out to the Lord for help (Romans 10:13).

Jesus doesn't demand that a person come to a particular system of organized religion, or to clean up their life and conquer all their faults. He doesn't require a person to wrap his brain around a complex philosophy of life full of do's and don'ts and boring activities. He says simply, "Come to Me as you are, acknowledging that you are broken and in need of fixing, and trust Me to start changing your life to become the way that it needs to be. Trust the fact that I died on the cross to pay the penalty for your sins, believing that God the Father is willing to count My death as a valid substitute for your punishment in your place. Believe that I rose from the dead. Ask God to forgive all your moral filth, trusting Me to give you the gift of eternal life."

Even though your message is simple, positive and free, people who hate God will still resist the truth. When that happens, persecution can be very costly and very painful.

But, hey, so what?

Pastor Polycarp

In the second century A.D., Roman authorities demanded that Pastor Polycarp stop telling people about the gospel of Christ. He refused. "Then we'll take all your possessions," they told him. "Go ahead," he replied. "My God will supply all I need." "We'll torture you," they threatened. "I would count it an honor to identify with the sufferings of my Lord," he said. "In that case, we'll kill you." Polycarp smiled, "That will be best of all, for to me, to live is Christ, and to die is gain. Nothing could be more wonderful!"

What a dilemma! How can you threaten a man with going to heaven? In frustration, not knowing what to do with such a courageous man, the Romans killed him. His boldness in his martyrdom only inspired thousands of other Christians to be fearless witnesses, just like him.

Forty Soldiers

At another time, a legion of Roman soldiers, of whom forty were Christians, were quartered for the winter in Northern Gaul [France] next to a frozen lake.[31] While there, an imperial decree was delivered to the general. All troops were required to worship the emperor of Rome.

The general, knowing the forty Christians in his

---

[31]These brave men are called the Forty Holy Martyrs of Sebaste; see http://www.mit.edu:8001/activities/ocf/sebaste_martyrs.html

regiment were his most valiant and courageous men, urged them to obey this command in order to save their lives.

In unison, the forty Christians said, "We cannot." The general was angry with them. To try to force them to comply, he ordered them to remove their uniforms and boots and to march out on to the ice naked, either until they froze to death, or until they changed their minds.

These brave forty Christian soldiers stripped off their clothing and marched out on to the frozen lake. As they marched, they sang this song: "Forty soldiers of Christ are we, and we will not deny our God; we fight for Thee, O Christ our King, and claim from Thee the crown."

Hour after hour they marched, all the while singing this song. Throughout this time, the general listened and wept, because he loved and respected these men.

Finally, the singing stopped. In a few minutes, one of the forty men had crawled back to the campfire, bloodied and bruised and frostbitten. In order to save his life, he was willing to bow his knee to the Emperor and submit to his demand. A few moments later, in the distance, the general heard a new song: "Thirty-nine soldiers of Christ are we, and we will not deny our God; we fight for Thee, O Christ our King, and claim from Thee the crown."

The general couldn't stand it any longer. He stripped off his own boots and clothing. He himself marched out on the ice toward the others, singing, "Forty soldiers of Christ are we, and we will not deny our God; we fight for Thee, O Christ our King, and claim from Thee the crown."

Are you a soldier of Christ? Is your commitment to Him strong enough that you would be willing to die for the One who died for you? Are you committed to be a witness for Jesus, even when it means sticking your neck out and taking an unpopular stand for Him?

In this brief window of time you have left on earth, what will you do to expand the kingdom of Christ? Now is the time for effective evangelism. Are you willing to witness for Christ?

Evangelism is not just a matter of "closing the deal." It includes everything you do to make faith in Christ an option for the unchurched. Every part of the process, from cultivating a friendship, to sowing a few seeds, to weeding out some false ideas, to harvesting the fruit, is crucial.

Perhaps God will call you to serve Him in a short-term missions trip in a poorer land. Perhaps He will ask you to sacrifice some creaturely comforts in order to help bring the gospel message to those who still have not heard the truth. Perhaps God will lead you into a ministry of prayer and intercession for the nations. Perhaps God will ask you to make a significantly large financial commitment to spread the gospel quickly to people living in the "10-40 Window" before the rapture strikes. The harvest is ripe now. But this day of opportunity will not last forever.

It's Your Choice

Here's how to start. Write down the names of people you know who need the Lord. Begin to pray for them on a regular basis. Ask God to touch their hearts and to open the doors for you to share Christ with them. Don't ask your pastor to visit them. You do it. As a lay person, you make the most effective witness. You are already scattered in the world, strategically located to witness in those pockets of our society that nobody else has access to. When you share your faith, people know that it's authentic, from your heart.

Don't sweat the possibility of persecution. Choose to invest your life in the mission and vision that Jesus Christ has given you to do. Take a risk. Spread gospel seeds among all the people you know. Gossip the gospel. In the short time you have left before Jesus Christ comes for you in the rapture and whisks you away from planet earth, go for the gold! Take a moment now to pray. Ask the Lord how He wants you to respond to Him in this important area of witnessing for Him. Then turn the page and record your responses on your second Personal Applicational Review.

◆ PERSONAL APPLICATIONAL REVIEW ◆

1. What is Christ's command to all Christians in His Great Commission?   "_____   _____" List the three parts of this process: _____ ing, _____ ing,_____ ing.

2. Underline your personal present passion level for witnessing:
Feverish!   Urgent   Important   Someday ...   Scared   Forget it!
Circle the passion level you want to be at by the end of this year.

3. What do you believe is true about hell? It is . . . Forever/torment?
Temporary/annihilation?   Everyone eventually goes to heaven?
Write a verse that supports your view: _____

4. Underline the ingredient for witnessing that is strongest for you:
Spiritual   Knowledgeable   Reasonable   Personable   Gentle   Respectful
Circle the ingredient for witnessing that you need to develop the most.

5. What's the worst persecution you have ever received as a Christian?

_____

On a scale of 1 (easy) to 10 (horrible), how bad was the experience?_____   What level (1 to 10) are you willing to endure to win others to Christ? _____

6. Write down names of three friends you want to share Christ with:

_____   _____   _____

Please take two minutes right now to pray for each of these three friends by name. You may want to use these words:

"Lord, I want to be a witness who is confident, convincing and conscientious for You. I pray that You will teach me to communicate my convictions about You more clearly and more boldly than ever before. I pray that You will use me to lead one of these three friends to faith in Jesus Christ sometime this year. In Jesus' name, Amen."

Section Three

WORSHIP Until Christ Comes

Ayoung boy from an unchurched home was on vacation in another state. His aunt was driving him through town. Pointing to a large church with a steeple, she said, "That is St. Paul's Church." The boy grimaced in reply, "It must be a franchise. We have one of those in our town, too."

Children can provide enlightening insights and fresh perception about church and God. One young girl, after challenged by her Sunday School teacher to write a letter to God, wrote, "Dear God, I had a good time at church today. Wish You could have been there. Love, Amber."

Is God present when you worship Him in your church or at home? Really?

Then why is it that spending 60 minutes in church seems so long when that same amount of time seems so short when golfing, fishing, or playing pinochle? Why does $20 looks so big in the offering plate but so small at the grocery store? Why is reading a few chapters in the Bible such a chore when devouring a novel is a breeze? Why is praying for ten minutes so difficult when you're a person who can easily sit and chat on the phone for hours? Why do you question what the Bible says, but believe what the newspaper says?

Strange, isn't it?

Have you seen the new hymnal with honest song titles? It includes "I Surrender Some," "Oh, How I Like Jesus," "When Peace Like A Trickle," and "Pillow of Ages,

Fluffed for Me."

We nervously chuckle because those titles are so convicting, revealing what's in our hearts.

I think it's time we got serious about worship. Don't you?

Is Jesus Christ ruling at the center of your life? Does He hold sole rights to your soul? If not, your priorities are out of whack. Your life will be consumed with trivial, temporal things that are shallow and earthbound. If you want to live a purpose-driven, meaningful life, you must learn to love and worship your Creator and Lord with all your heart, mind, soul and strength.

Deep within every human heart is a restless hunger and yearning to be in the presence of unconditional love and power. The only way that primal longing can be filled, the only way your personal heart wounds can be healed, is by you learning to worship in the presence of a holy God.

The Bible instructs us to prepare for Christ's return through worship. In 1 Corinthians 11:26, Paul says that we are to worship the Lord within our churches through participating in the bread and cup of communion "until he comes."

What does it mean to worship? The word "worship" originally was two words: "worth-ship." The compound word means "to declare the worth of God." Worship is God-centered adoration that attributes to Him the highest worth through praise and prayer. Worship is the response of your whole person to the presence, promises and power of God. It is a willingness to surrender and sacrifice all that you are, and all that you have, for His glory.

In the book of Revelation, descriptions of the worship of God in heaven (Revelation 4-5 and 20-22) function as bookends that bracket the Bible's descriptions of the wrath of God on earth (Revelation 6-19). In Revelation 4:10-11, God the Father is worshiped as Creator and Sustainer. In Revelation 5:8-14, God the Son is worshiped as Redeemer and King. By reading Revelation 21-22, you can enjoy a sweet foretaste of the ecstasy of worshiping God forever.

If you are a Christian, you are in the process of becoming more and more like Jesus Christ. That is God's prime objective–to form, conform and transform your life to fit the image, the character, of His Firstborn Son (Romans 8:29). As you worship Jesus Christ, God does surgery on your soul. He bends your mind, emotions and will to change the way you think, feel and behave.

Before God's Word can take root in your life to bloom, grow and produce fruit in you, your heart must be tilled and cultivated to become receptive to the seed. God uses your worship of Him to transform the hard and frozen ground in your heart into soft and sandy fertile soil.

Worship is not just a matter of warm-fuzzy sensations or tears or big time tingles. The Bible teaches that in order to worship God with all your heart, four things must be true in your life.

Let's walk through these four aspects of worship in the next four chapters.

"Let us not give up meeting
together, as some are
in the habit of doing."

✦ Chapter 10 ✦

Serve God in a Local Church

I am astounded at the number of unchurched Christians in America. Millions of people profess faith in Christ, but want nothing to do with His church. Are you one of them? Or do you understand that you need to worship God in a local church each Sunday (or Saturday)?

There are at least four good reasons to make "church" a weekly priority in your life.

God's Kingdom

One, Jesus is determined to build His kingdom through local churches. God intends for every believer to function as part of a church within his own community. God does not want you to be a "floating" saint who hops and shops between churches. He wants you to settle down in a church where you can link arms with others to accomplish God's work in your community. Just as every basketball player joins a team, and every soldier joins a platoon, and every worker joins a company, so God calls every Christian to join a local church and be part of a spiritual team.

Personal Renewal

Two, you need a local church because after a week full of stressful, exhausting activity, you need a spiritual day of rest. You need a change of pace. You need to stop running at your usual frantic speed and, for at least an hour, pause long enough to look your Creator full in the face. You need to ponder His glory in order to refresh your perspective and renew your spiritual strength and be challenged to apply God's Word before you head out to tackle the next week.

Group Praise

Three, you need a larger group of people in church to help you regain a vision for how big God really is. Times of corporate worship, singing songs that stir your soul and lift your spirit, are needed to help you feel overwhelmed by the greatness of God's presence, promises and power.

Mutual Encouragement

Four, God commands you to love, serve, teach, encourage and exhort one another on a consistent basis. You can't do that without a local church. Hebrews 10:24-25 clearly states:

> And let us consider how we may spur one another on toward love and good deeds. Let us not give up meeting together, as some are in the habit of doing, but let us encourage one another—and all the more as you see the Day approaching.

In view of the evidences that Christ's return is near, Christians are to meet together to encourage and stimulate one another to love and good deeds within a Bible-teaching church. If you are not involved regularly in a Christ-centered local church, you are living outside of God's will.

What To Do In Church

Hebrews 13:15-16 instructs us about worship:

> Through Jesus, therefore, let us continually offer to God a sacrifice of praise—the fruit of lips that confess his name. And do not forget to do good and to share with others, for with such sacrifices God is pleased.

When you come to a church service, do you halfheartedly mumble through the songs, daydream during the sermon, and then drop five bucks in the offering plate? If so, you haven't truly worshiped. Or, do you energetically sing praises to God, pay attention during the sermon, give back to God a substantial portion of your income, and volunteer to serve in the nursery once a month?

If so, you have demonstrated your love for God through acts of sacrifice that please Him.

Is Jesus Christ worth such sacrifices? He died to redeem your soul from an eternity in hell. What sacrifice on your part could be too great to make for Him? He deserves much more than your mediocrity, shortcuts, leftovers and excuses. He is worthy of receiving your very best. As Revelation 4:11 affirms, "You are worthy, our Lord and God, to receive glory and honor and power, for you created all things, and by your will they were created and have their being."

Jesus Christ is worthy of your worship. God created you so that you would love Him and glorify Him forever. That is your purpose for living. Each week, you are given the awesome privilege of gathering together with other people like you who will live forever to worship the sovereign Lord who controls your destiny.

Think about your worship in church as a dress rehearsal for worship in heaven. Revelation 5:11-14 describes how it will be when all heaven breaks loose with continual praise:

> Then I looked and heard the voice of many angels, numbering thousands upon thousands, and ten thousand times ten thousand. They encircled the throne and the living creatures and the elders. In a loud voice they sang: 'Worthy is the Lamb, who was slain, to receive power and wealth and wisdom and strength and honor and glory and praise!' Then I heard every creature in heaven and on earth and under the earth and on the sea, and all that is in them, singing: 'To him who sits on the throne and to the Lamb be praise and honor and glory and power, for ever and ever!' The four living creatures said, 'Amen,' and the elders fell down and worshiped.

In view of Christ's coming, why should you worship Him? One, He died to protect you from the justice of God's holy wrath in the horror of eternal hell fire (Revelation 14:9-11; 20:10-15). Two, He has promised to deliver you from the future, universal hour of trial that will punish all earth-dwellers (Revelation 3:10; 1 Thessalonians 5:9; Revelation 14:17-20; 16:5-7). Three, He loves you so much that He insists on marrying you as His Bride (Revelation

19:7).

Be painfully honest with yourself about this. What weakens your worship the most?

Weak Worship #1

One culprit may be the disease of "spectatoritus." Do you tend to regard worship as a spectator sport, something you do by going to church to watch and listen to others worship the Lord? Do you sit in your pew thinking that the singing and the offering are mere "preliminaries" to the preaching, just "opening exercises" to fill in the time before the "main event"? If so, you have missed the whole point of being there. If you walk out of church saying to yourself, "I didn't get anything out of it today," your thinking is completely on the wrong wavelength.

Worship is not supposed to be a time of you getting something for yourself. It is a time for you giving yourself to God so that He gets something out of it.

Hit the Court!

At every basketball game, there are three main groups of people, the players, the coaches and the spectators. Imagine a church service to be like a basketball game. Given that analogy, a lot of Christians assume that the people on the platform are the players, that God is their coach, and that the congregation is the audience who has come to watch the game from the stands.

Wrong! That is totally backwards from the way God designed it to be.

In reality, the congregation is the players on the court; those who serve on the platform are the coaches; and God is the audience of One. You are not sitting in the grandstands, watching it happen. You are on the basketball court, making it happen. God is in the grandstands of heaven watching your heart to see how well you rebound, dribble, pass and shoot, as you worship Him!

The next time you attend your church, don't go to

receive a spiritual handout or to be entertained. Go for the purpose of giving God your very best. Go not to spectate, but to participate with your heart fully in gear. Worship in the knowledge that God is watching and evaluating your performance as a worshiper. Worship with the goal that God will give you a standing ovation at the end of the service because He knows you gave all that you had for Him.

Weak Worship #2

A second culprit that may weaken your worship is that of being self-conscious instead of being God-conscious. When you are in church, do you fix your attention intently on your own problems, your own needs, and your own hurts, instead of on God? If so, it's no wonder you don't feel like worshiping God; you are secretly blaming God for your troubles. You are preoccupied with your own self-centered desires for health and wealth that He is not delivering at the moment.

When you are self-conscious, you become afraid that some onlooker will "catch" you in an act of genuine worship. You are mentally distracted by the thought of what others might think. This short-circuits the process of worshiping all together. A key to experiencing true worship is to switch from being self-conscious to being God-conscious. Learn how to put yourself on the shelf in order to become absorbed and pre-occupied with knowing, exalting and serving your God.

In a practical way, how can you make the time you spend in church less spectatorish, less self-conscious, and more worshipful? How can you give the Lord your undivided attention so that you can be fully conscious of how wonderful and worthy He is when you take the time to worship Him in church? Try following these seven specific suggestions.

Seven Suggestions

First, prepare your heart for worship by practicing the presence of God before the service begins. If you are a true Christian, God the Holy Spirit lives within you. You are a living, breathing, moving temple of God. The place where true worship occurs is not within a building, but within your body. Spend some time in the conscious awareness that God is with you, and communicate with Him in prayer from within your own heart.

Second, do your best to ignore all the distractions around you. Keep your thoughts focused on the Lord. When someone walks in late, or when a baby cries, discipline yourself not to turn around to look. Don't write notes, giggle, talk or plan out what you're going to do for dinner. When you open your Bible or hymnal, concentrate intently on the meaning of the words. When you sing a familiar chorus, close your eyes to concentrate on its meaning, or look up at the rafters and cast your gaze towards heaven, making it a song that you are personally singing to your Lord.

Third, when someone is leading in a public prayer, be an active participant in that prayer by piggybacking on it, silently echoing its words as your own. Don't just eavesdrop, listening in on another person's conversation with God. Rather, pray along, agreeing and affirming the spoken words to be your own personal prayer to God. Say "Amen" from your heart, silently repeating and echoing the words to make that prayer your own.[32]

---

[32]Prepare for this by spending time in prayer each day on your own. There are five types of prayer: praise, thanksgiving, confession, petition and intercession. God invites you to use all five kinds of prayer.

Real change in the world occurs not in the ballot box, not in the battle front, but in the prayer closet. God's promise in 2 Chronicles 7:14 is true: "if my people, who are called by my name, will humble themselves and pray and seek my face and turn from their wicked ways, then will I hear from heaven and will forgive their sin and will heal their land." If you really believed that, you might spend less time waving protest signs before men and more time "sucking carpet" before the Lord.

Fourth, turn your palms upwards to God as you sing or pray as a way of adoring Him. Perhaps you grew up in a church where the only acceptable reason for raising your hand in church is to ask a question of the teacher. If so, study what the Bible teaches about opening up your hands to God in worship (1 Timothy 2:8). This tiny act of sacrifice helps you engage your whole heart in genuine worship. You might feel a little awkward the first time you try it, but nothing conspicuous or sensational or bizarre will happen. You won't fall to the floor speaking in tongues. But you will be surprised how a simple twist of the wrists can quickly put your heart in tune with the wonder of worshiping God. The point of doing it is not to try to artificially produce spiritual goose bumps, but to help nudge yourself a bit closer to the reality of worshiping God from your heart.

Fifth, when it comes to giving, give sacrificially. Invest heavily in your local church ministry. Your church, more than anything else you are associated with, can make a difference for eternity. Don't pawn off on God your leftovers, your second best, your hand-me-downs. Give generously out of a conviction that Jesus Christ is worthy of the very best you have to give. If you have not been tithing, increase your giving until it is at least ten percent.

Sixth, worship Christ by participating regularly in the Lord's Supper. 1 Corinthians 11:26 teaches that we are to participate in a meaningful observance of the Lord's Supper "until He comes." Use the quietness of communion to humble your heart before the Lamb of God who was slain for your sins. Focus on how Jesus Christ gave Himself to be mutilated and slaughtered as a sacrificial animal for you. Dwell on the gore of thorns in His skull, a whip lacerating His back, fists hitting His face, nails gouging His hands, and a spear tearing open His side. Let the tears come to your eyes as you meditate on Jesus absorbing the full wrath of God for your rebellious crimes. He was crushed, smitten, afflicted, pierced, scourged, and oppressed for your iniquities. The nail holes through His wrists and feet still scar and disfigure His glorified body as eternal visual reminders of how much He loves you.[33] The Lord's Supper, whose purpose is to vividly remind you of the horror of the crucifixion, is an element of worship that can only take place within the context of a Bible-believing local church.

Seventh, when the gospel is preached, glory in what Christ has done for you on the cross. Think about the fact that if Christ had not gone to Calvary, you would have gone to hell. Before you can truly appreciate the glorious honor of heaven, you must first pause to comprehend the gruesome horror of hell. The amazing truth is that Christ loves you so much that He chose to suffer the miseries of hell in your place. So humble yourself before the holiness of Christ, the Holy One who gave up His life so you could live. Praise Him for the privilege of being part of "the church of God, which he bought with his own blood" (Acts 20:28).

This weekend, focus on following these seven guidelines. Your experience of God's presence and power will be richer for it. And that will help you to grasp the importance of Chapter 11.

---

[33] Steven J. Lawson, *Heaven Help Us!* (Colorado Springs, CO: NavPress, 1995), 76. Page 77 tells the story of a Sunday School teacher who asked "Is there anything manmade in heaven?" "Yes," a little boy answered. "The nail prints in Jesus' hands."

◆ Chapter 11 ◆

Focus on the Glory of Christ

In order to be motivated to hear and obey what Christ has to say to you through His Church on earth, you need to fully grasp the glory of Christ's sovereign Lordship in heaven.

In Revelation 1:5-6, the Apostle John graphically describes seven glorious truths about Jesus Christ as He is right now. Let's focus our sights on each one:

> Jesus Christ, who is the faithful witness, the firstborn from the dead, and the ruler of the kings of the earth. To him who loves us and has freed us from our sins by his blood, and has made us to be a kingdom and priests to serve his God and Father–to him be glory and power for ever and ever! Amen.

The Revealer

First, Jesus Christ is the revealer. All He says is true. In this confusing world, you are bombarded by conflicting philosophies that are antagonistic to each other. You often wonder, "Which is right?" The answer is found on the lips of the faithful witness, the totally credible One who perfectly reveals the Father to you and who explains the absolute truth about life.

The Resurrected One

Second, Christ is the resurrected One. Jesus is the first and only person to ever yet rise in glory through the resurrection from the dead, never to die again. He is the firstborn from the dead, the firstfruits of a great harvest from the dead that is yet to come.

The Ruler

Third, Christ is the ruler. The future of this planet is not dependent on decisions made by powerful leaders in the United Nations, in the Middle East or in the White House. Jesus Christ is the sovereign Lord who sets limits on their power. He is the king over all other kings. If they are not submissive to Him, they are being insubordinate and will one day have to pay the penalty of their rebellion against His righteous rule.

The Reassurer

Fourth, Christ is the reassurer. The phrase "to him who loves us" is stated in the present tense. Jesus loves you at this moment. Even though He knows that you are faithless, foolish, arrogant, sinful and selfish, still He loves you right now.

The Redeemer

Fifth, Christ is the redeemer. Christ has broken the shackles of your worst evil habits, setting you free from those sins that used to harass and limit your life, and freed you with His blood. As the hymn "O For A Thousand Tongues" articulates so well, "He breaks the power of cancelled sin, He sets the prisoner free; His blood can make the foulest clean; His blood availed for me!"

The Recruiter

Sixth, Christ is the recruiter. Jesus Christ has recruited you to "be a kingdom and priests to serve his God and Father." A priest is a professional worshipper. 1 Peter 2:5 reminds you that even now you are part of "a holy priesthood, offering spiritual sacrifices acceptable to God through Jesus Christ." God wants your whole life to be devoted to worshiping Him. That is your job.

The Reason for Living

Seventh, Christ is the reason for living. The reason you exist is to glorify Christ forever. The bottom-line purpose of your life is to please Him by becoming more like Him each day.

This seven-fold glorious Jesus Christ is about to reveal Himself to the apostle John in a vision. It had been sixty-two years since John last saw his Lord. When John hears His voice, he jumps out of his skin. His hair stands on end. Quickly he turns to see His beloved Lord Jesus.[34]

John describes seven parts of Jesus' glorified appearance in Revelation 1:14-16:

> His head and hair were white like wool, as white as snow, and his eyes were like blazing fire. His feet were like bronze glowing in a furnace, and his voice was like the sound of rushing waters. In his right hand he held seven stars, and out of his mouth came a sharp double-edged sword. His face was like the sun shining in all its brilliance.

This is not the same kind of picture of Jesus you see in children's storybooks. After He ascended to heaven, Jesus has definitely changed His looks!

What does it all mean?

First, Jesus' white head and hair speaks of His absolute purity, reminding us that Jesus never sinned. 2 Corinthians 5:21 says Christ "knew no sin." Hebrews 4:15 states that He was "without sin." Pilate declared after examining Him, "I find no fault in Him."

Second, Jesus has fiery lasers flashing out of each eye socket. His eyes are like flaming red searchlights with a penetrating, piercing gaze. Hebrews 4:13 states, "Nothing in all creation is hidden from God's sight. Everything is uncovered and laid bare before the eyes of Him to whom we must give account." Absolutely nothing can be hidden from Him, not even the deepest motives of your heart. Jesus sees every detail about you with X-ray vision. With penetrating insight, He is continually watching and

---

[34] I am deeply indebted to Steven J. Lawson's *Final Call.* (Westchester, IL: Crossway Books, 1994) for many of the descriptive phrases used in this section.

evaluating everything you say, think and do.

Third, Jesus' "feet were like bronze." Bronze was the material that composed the temple "brazen" altar. On it, all sin offerings were sacrificed. This speaks of God's burning anger against sin and His execution of righteous judgment against those who rebel against His righteous rule.

Fourth, Jesus speaks with a loud voice. It is like the deafening roar of a waterfall plummeting hundreds of feet below, as the cascading waters completely drown out all you try to say. When Christ speaks, He drowns out all other voices. His truth flushes away man's feeble opinions. His words cannot be refuted. His appraisals cannot be debated. His verdicts cannot be overturned.

Fifth, Jesus' hand "held seven stars." These stars, representing God's messengers to His churches (perhaps pastors), are in the palm of Jesus' hand. Being in Christ's hand means that He controls and protects them. He holds the whole world in His hands, but pastors who serve as His messengers to His people are especially precious to Him.

Sixth, Jesus' mouth contains "a sharp double-edged sword." This sword portrays Christ's judicial authority to discipline His Church, removing ungodly attitudes, bringing conviction that leads to repentance. With His sharp sword, Jesus stands ready to surgically remove sin from His body like a surgeon is ready to cut out a life-threatening malignancy. The Great Physician wants to cut out of your life those malignancies that are making you spiritually sick. Hebrews 4:12 says:

> For the word of God is living and active. Sharper than any double-edged sword, it penetrates even to dividing soul and spirit, joints and marrow; it judges the thoughts and attitudes of the heart.

Seventh, Jesus' "face was like the sun shining in all its brilliance." When you look up at the sun shining in all its strength, you can see nothing else. Similarly, Jesus Christ is the focal point of the universe, the cosmic center of all of life. His face shines like the sun, too brilliant to look upon, for it radiates with the splendor and majesty of the Shekinah glory of God.

What a vision of Christ! His head, eyes, feet, voice, hand, mouth, and face, all portray perfect power and authority. Jesus Christ is no longer a lowly, suffering servant on a cross. He is now our risen and victorious King of Kings, utterly gleaming in glory and greatness.

Your Image of Him

When you close your eyes to pray, is this the Christ you see? When you confess your sin, is it this Lord before whom you kneel? When you worship, is this the Jesus to whom you sing? When you read your Bible, is it this Master that you hear speaking to you?

Probably not. But why?

Perhaps you have become too casual in your relationship with Christ, too comfortable, too horizontal, too "buddy-buddy." In a recent survey of ex-church members, it was revealed that the main reason they stopped going to church was that they found it "boring."

Boring? Not this Christ! This Christ reigns in exalted loftiness, dwells in consuming majesty and rules in transcendent glory. There is nothing boring about Him at all!

Let's suppose that this Jesus whom you have just read about were to walk into your church next Sunday. What would be your response? Would you keep singing? Would you walk over to Him and introduce yourself? Would you invite Him to sit next to you and share your hymnal? Would you ask Him to explain some mystery that has been perplexing you? Would you run over and hug Him? Would you ask Him to autograph your Bible?

No way. You wouldn't do any of those things.

What you would do is immediately fall on your face before Him. Covering your eyes from the glare of His glory, you would drop to the ground in humble adoration. With fear and trembling, you would acknowledge His divine presence by collapsing to the floor, falling to the ground like cut timber. Holy terror would grip your heart. You would experience genuine repentance and revival like you've never before known. Your face would hit the dirt, and you would experience complete brokenness before Him.

Flat On Your Face

That is exactly what happened to John when he saw Christ face to face. Revelation 1:17 records, "When I saw him, I fell at his feet as though dead." Instantly, John collapsed to the ground. Every nerve fiber in his body was trembling. He felt terrified and overwhelmed. He buried his face in the dirt before his Lord.

Why? Because in that split second, John saw his own sinful depravity. The holiness of Christ exposed man's unholiness. The aged apostle, haggard and emaciated, was looking upon unveiled Deity. No one can stand erect in the presence of a holy God, not even the great apostle John.

Between Christ's holiness and your unholiness is an infinite gulf. Until you see His holiness, you will never know the depth of your own sin. When you compare yourself with other people, you seem fairly respectable. But when you compare yourself to Him, you are shaken down to your roots! The closer you draw to the Light, the more dirt in your own heart is exposed to view.

As John lies limp at Jesus' feet, an omnipotent hand reaches out to restore his disintegrated soul. It is a touch of tender grace that brings reassuring comfort and peace to this elderly apostle. Jesus then reassured him. "Do not be afraid."

Jesus revealed to John who He was by saying, "'I am the First and the Last'" (Revelation 1:17). As "the First," Christ lays claim to eternal preexistence (John 1:1-3). As "the Last," Christ claims to be eternally immutable. From everlasting to everlasting, He is God, the same "yesterday, today and forever" (Hebrews 13:8).

God invites you to keep your eyes fixed and focused on the glory of your perfect and powerful Savior so that you will wholeheartedly worship Him. When you do, it will be much more natural to surrender to His Lordship in every area of your life.

Are you ready?

Let's look at that next.

Dare to be a disciplined disciple
who lives to please the Lord.

◆ *Chapter 12* ◆

Yield to Christ's Lordship

Worship is incomplete until you make a one-time crisis decision to yield your entire life to the Lordship of Jesus Christ. In fact, to do anything less than totally submit and surrender your life to serve God is to slap God in the face with ingratitude for all the mercy He has shown to you.

Romans 12:1 says to you:

> Therefore, I urge you, brothers, in view of God's mercy, to offer your bodies as living sacrifices, holy and pleasing to God–this is your spiritual act of worship.

God expects you to present your body as a sacrifice to Him. You may think, "God doesn't really want my body. It has B.O., it snores, it has warts and moles in places you don't want to know about. Parts of it are really ugly and old. You don't really want this body, Lord, do you?"

Yes, God says that He does. But why is He interested in your body? Why doesn't Paul say, "offer your spirit and soul to God"? It is because the body is the last frontier of surrender. God knows that if you give your body to Him, everything else will follow naturally.

What does God want you to do with your body? Present it to Him as a sacrifice! Offer it wholeheartedly to Him, placing your entire self at God's disposal to do with you exactly as He sees fit. God wants you to yield your rights to Him and allow Him to rule your life. He wants your total, unquestioning submission to obey Christ as your Lord. He wants you to surrender all your selfishness and pride.

Self Sacrifice

God gives four specifics about this sacrifice of self that

He expects from you.

One, this sacrifice is living. God doesn't want a dead sacrifice that He can mount in a trophy case. He wants a living sacrifice that will take His gospel to a world that desperately needs to hear the truth about Jesus Christ. Because a living sacrifice has a tendency to keep crawling off the altar, this sacrifice needs to be renewed repeatedly. Each day, acknowledge that you are God's property forever. You no longer belong to yourself. You no longer have the right to run your own life.

Two, this sacrifice is holy. It sets you apart to serve God in humility and moral purity. It surrenders your body to be sanctified and conformed to the character and conduct of Jesus Christ.

Three, this sacrifice is pleasing to God. It brings maximum joy to His heart. As 2 Corinthians 5:9 states, "we make it our goal to please him." Pleasing God is to be the top priority of your life.

Four, this sacrifice is reasonable. It is logical and rational, the only proper choice for a child of God to make. In light of what God has done for you, total commitment to obey God makes perfect sense. The only other alternative is disobedience, and that would be unreasonable. Why? Because as a Christian, you have been redeemed by the priceless blood of Christ. You already belong to God. He paid for you. You are His. If you fail to give your entire self back to God, you are guilty of robbing God because you are holding back from Him something that is rightfully His - the sacrifice of your will to God's superior will.

Not Conformed

When you surrender your will to God's, your life changes in two ways. Romans 12:2 explains, "Do not conform any longer to the pattern of this world, but be transformed by the renewing of your mind."

The phrase "do not conform" sounds negative. Does it mean that as a Christian, you don't smoke, don't chew, don't drink, don't dance, don't gamble, don't attend theaters, and if you want to be really spiritual, sell your TV set and never drink coffee or eat pork again?

Unfortunately, some people imagine they obey this verse by merely following a list of forbidden activities. But you cannot avoid being conformed to this world through a list of don'ts. That never works. It is possible to give up on all these worldly things and still be saturated with the spirit of materialism, sensuality, pride and bitterness.

So, what does Paul mean when he commands, "do not be conformed to this world"?

The "world" refers to the values and attitudes and activities of the contemporary society in which we live. So it means you stop allowing your activities, attitudes and values to be patterned after those of contemporary society. It means you don't let the world around you squeeze you into its mold. It means you learn to recognize the subtle, systematic brainwashing that is continually thrust at you by the world's media, and consciously refuse to adapt to it.

For example, the philosophy of the world states, "You deserve a break today;" "Do it your way;" "How could it be wrong if it feels so right?" The world teaches that there are no absolutes, that you have total freedom to do what is right in your own eyes, and that "whatever you believe is right for you." But that is all wrong.

The world claims that it is okay to lie to get by, to disrespect your parents, to cheat on your taxes, to live together without marriage, to swear and cuss, to pursue the latest material possessions with a constant lust for more, to fill your mind with R-rated movies, to hold bitter grudges against people, to be selfish with your money, and to seek personal pleasure and fun as your life's highest goal. But all these worldly ways are sinfully distorted.

Most likely, non-biblical values echo within your mind so frequently that if you are not vigilant, you will soon adopt these garbage ideas as your own. Gradually and subtly, you will end up making decisions on the basis of wrong values and unbiblical philosophies, without even realizing what's happening.

If you were to suddenly start carrying a twenty-pound ball strapped to your stomach, you would know that something was definitely wrong. You would act to change it immediately. But if you were to add just a few pounds a year, very gradually, you would begin to think that being twenty pounds overweight was normal. You would become used to it. Instead of fighting it, you would just adapt to it, and assume "that's the way it is." Worldly values gradually accumulate in your mind in a similar way.

Be Transformed

How do you resist this slow, insidious process of being pressed into the world's mold? God says you must gradually change your way of thinking by replacing wrong ideas with right ideas. You must exchange false values for true values. You need a positive transformation.

How? It happens through the renewing of your mind.

Your mind is like a sponge. It soaks up whatever information and values you expose it to on a regular basis and adapts to it. If you normally spend twenty or thirty hours a week in front of the TV set, but only one hour a week in church, and no time during the week for personal Bible reading, from which source do you expect your values to come?

Take a wild guess. Will your thinking gradually become more biblical or more worldly?

That's your problem, isn't it? Be completely honest with yourself. From which sources does your mind pick up most of its impressions? Remember, your mind will adapt itself to, and mold itself around, those ethics, values and behaviors that you expose it to the most.

God wants to transform your mind. The word "transformed" in Greek is "metamorphosis." It describes a process of being changed from one form to another. For example, a small furry, many-legged caterpillar is "metamorphosed" into a beautiful, transparent-winged butterfly. In a similar way, you are "metamorphosed" when you allow the Holy Spirit to remold and renew your attitudes and thinking patterns by means of a continual, conscious absorption of the Word of God.

The only way to protect your mind from being attacked by worldly false values is to develop a keen sense of spiritual perceptiveness. How? By increasing your daily intake of biblical truth, learning to think God's thoughts after Him.

This process occurs in five ways. You hear the Word, read the Word, study the Word, memorize the Word and meditate on the Word. Each of these five ways takes time and conscious work, but each one is essential to renew your mind to think like Jesus Christ thinks.

A "living sacrifice" surrender to the Lordship of Christ will result in positive life-change. As you consciously and continually absorb Scripture into your mind, your way of thinking will be renewed, and that will change the way you feel and act.

When one's mind is renewed, a teenager will quickly do what he is told without arguing about "why." A husband will occasionally volunteer to take his wife out to dinner. A wife will shower her husband with words of praise and respect. You'll look forward to your Home Bible Study each week. You'll start giving thanks instead of becoming discouraged. The very thought of lying, swearing, hating, cheating, lusting or coveting will become abhorrent to you. You'll become a person who is happier, easier to live with, and worthy of high respect.

How? It all results from the continual, daily renewing of your mind through an increased conscious absorption of God's Word.

Knowing God's Will

The renewing of your mind will result in the very practical benefit of knowing the will of God. Romans 12:2

promises, "Then you will be able to test and approve what God's will is, his good, pleasing and perfect will."

The words "test and approve" refer to putting God's will to the test and finding it to be true in your own experience. You will discover that God's will never fails, is never wrong, and that you can confidently trust it without reservation.

Contrary to popular belief, the "will of God" is not as confusing and obscure as a mystery novel. God wants you to know and experience God's will with absolute certainty and assurance. How? By reading, believing and applying what is so clearly revealed to you in the Word of God! Once you commit yourself to the renewal of your mind, you will want to find out what the Word of God says so that you can obey it. As you do, you will prove in your own experience that God's will is good, pleasing and perfect.

But remember, before any of this can happen in your experience, you must yield to the Lordship of Christ. You must surrender yourself totally to God as a living sacrifice.

You must dare to be a disciplined disciple.

Cortez landed at Vera Cruz in 1519 to begin his conquest of Mexico. With only a small force of seven hundred men, he purposely set fire to his fleet of eleven ships. On the shore, his men watched in horror as their only means of retreat sank to the bottom of the Gulf of Mexico. With no means of retreat, there was only one direction to move, forward into the Mexican interior to meet whatever might come their way.

If you are serious about being Christ's disciple, you must purposefully destroy all avenues of retreat. You must resolve that whatever the price is to be His follower, you are willing to pay it. You will be a living sacrifice for Him. You will surrender and submit to His Lordship once and for all, then never look back. And you will seek to be filled with the Holy Spirit each day.

Hang on! That's next!

✦ Chapter 13 ✦

Be Filled with the Holy Spirit

Your worship is incredibly valuable to God. According to the Scriptures, a worshipping person is the only thing that God ever seeks. In John 4:23-24, Jesus announces:

Yet a time is coming and has now come when the true worshipers will worship the Father in spirit and truth, for they are the kind of worshipers the Father seeks. God is spirit, and his worshipers must worship in spirit and in truth.

To worship in truth (as seen in Romans 12:1-2) means to be guided by the objective truth of God's written Word, staying immersed in His truth. To worship in spirit means to make the continual choice to be filled with the Holy Spirit, daily yielding to His control over your life.

Ephesians 5:18 commands, "Do not get drunk on wine, which leads to debauchery. Instead, be filled with the Spirit." Worship involves a lifestyle habit of being filled with the Spirit each day.

Being filled with the Spirit could be called "spiritual intoxication," for it involves your being controlled by a continual consent to obey the leading of the Spirit. A person who is drunk with wine is a person who is being controlled by the alcohol within him. The alcohol that fills his body changes his thought-patterns, changes his speech, changes his actions, and causes him to do certain things which are normally unnatural for him to do. It causes untypical behavior. In a similar way, when a person is filled with the Spirit, he is "under the influence" of the Spirit within him. He will act, speak, and think differently than "normal" people.

Paul's comparison is, "Do not place yourself under the influence of alcoholic spirits, but do place yourself under the influence of The Spirit."

Filling Instructions

Being filled with the Spirit is not a once-for-all event. A drunkard doesn't get drunk once and stay that way forever. Instead, he drinks every day, perhaps several times a day. Since the effects of his drinking eventually wear off, he must keep on drinking in order to stay drunk.

In a similar way, a Spiritaholic Christian needs to keep on being re-filled with the Spirit in order to keep on being Spirit-filled. Ephesians 5:18, literally translated, states, "keep on being filled with the Spirit" or "continue being filled with the Spirit."

To worship Christ as a Spirit-filled Christian, you need to be filled with the Spirit each day. No Christian can live on the steam of yesterday's spiritual power. As soon as you become conscious of the fact that you have sinned, and that your own ego has temporarily mutinied against the Spirit's control in your life, you need to be re-filled with the Spirit, perhaps several times a day.

Nowhere in Scripture is there a verse that announces, "here is how to be filled with the Holy Spirit." However, by examining the New Testament commands concerning our relationship with the Holy Spirit, we can discern two key conditions that are essential for the filling of the Holy Spirit. These two key conditions, which you should brand on your brain forever, are the words cleansing and control.

Be Cleansed Through Repentance

The Holy Spirit is a Person with feelings, and when we sin, we hurt Him emotionally. Ephesians 4:30 explains that in order to be filled with the Spirit, you need to be cleansed from your sin. "And do not grieve the Holy Spirit of God, with whom you were sealed for the day of redemption." When you grieve the Spirit, you are not filled with Him. To grieve the Holy Spirit is to make Him feel sad or to cause him to be sorrowful because of your sin (Ephesians 4:25-5:4). It is to cause Him to wince at your careless living, your improper speech, or your grudges and bitterness against people whom God wants you to forgive. All of these sins hurt His heart.

As a Christian, the Holy Spirit lives inside your body like a houseguest living inside of your home. Think of how He feels when you argue and scream at your family members, or when you harbor resentment against past offenses. Imagine how shocked, embarrassed and disappointed He feels when you swear or gossip or steal something that's not yours. Realize how awful it is for Him when, for entertainment, you watch immoral scenes and laugh at filthy jokes on movies and TV.

All of your sinful thoughts, attitudes, words and behaviors grieve the heart of the Spirit of God who lives inside of you. Your sin pushes Him away from the center of your life. When you grieve Him, He cannot control your life, and as a result, you cannot experience His power.

When you realize that you are not filled with the Holy Spirit, you must be cleansed on the inside by confessing your sin to God. 1 John 1:9 promises, "If we confess our sins, he is faithful and just and will forgive us our sins and purify us from all unrighteousness."

What sins of omission (what you know you should but don't do) do you have to confess? They might include ingratitude, lack of love for God, neglect of Bible study, neglect of prayer, failure to attend church, lack of willingness to witness and serve, neglect of family responsibilities, not being hospitable, and refusal to deny yourself.

What sins of commission (what you know you shouldn't do but do anyway) do you have to confess? They might include worldliness, pride, envy, bitterness, materialism, hypocrisy, lust, slander, gossip, lying, cheating, robbing God, and failure to control your temper.

Before you can be filled with God's Spirit, your particular sins must be confessed, renounced and put behind you. As you deepen your worship of the Lord, you will develop an increasingly keen sensitivity to sin. You will learn to practice instant confession. As you mature in Christ, the time lapse between your sin and your confession will grow shorter and shorter. You may even arrive at the place where you can "catch" yourself early and stop short of sinning.

You will never become sinless, but over time, you should sin less and less.

To be cleansed, you must repent from your sin before God. Repentance means turning from your past mistakes and deciding in your heart not to repeat those same mistakes again.

When you realize that you are not filled with the Spirit, but want to be, the first thing you need is to be cleansed. The second thing you need is to be controlled.

Be Controlled Through Surrender

Paul speaks of the importance of being controlled by the Spirit in Galatians 5:16-18:

> So I say, live by the Spirit, and you will not gratify the desires of the sinful nature. For the sinful nature desires what is contrary to the Spirit, and the Spirit what is contrary to the sinful nature. They are in conflict with each other, so that you do not do what you want. But if you are led by the Spirit, you are not under law.

To live by the Spirit is to surrender to the Holy Spirit's control, to live each moment in conscious submission to do the Spirit's will. When He uncovers a new pocket of self-centeredness in your life, it is to admit, "Yes Lord, I have been trying to run that part of my life independently from you. From now on, I want not my will, but Your will to be done in my life." It is to visualize yourself being plugged into the Holy Spirit, your power-source, without whom you would be as helpless as an electric skill-saw on a pack trip.

It means actively trusting Him to do for you and through you what you admit you can't do for yourself.

God's two conditions for being filled with the Holy Spirit are cleansing and control. You are cleansed by the Holy Spirit when you confess your sin. You are controlled by the Holy Spirit when you surrender yourself completely to obey the Spirit's will.

Being Spirit-filled is not a matter of you getting more of the Spirit. It's a matter of the Spirit getting all of you.

Worshiping Christ, in view of His coming, is a matter of continually, consciously seeing Him at the center of every part of your life. Such worship involves serving Him within a local church, focusing on Christ's glory, yielding to Christ's Lordship, and daily submitting to being filled with the Holy Spirit. Do you worship Christ in these four ways?

When you worship God like this, the results are world-changing. Christ is glorified, the Church is unified, believers are edified, the lost are evangelized and the devil is terrified. So, what are you waiting for? Take time to worship Him right now.

Part of your worship includes taking an honest personal inventory of where you are and then setting a course for where you want to be. So, go ahead and use the third Personal Applicational Review on the next page to help you do just that.

✦ PERSONAL APPLICATIONAL REVIEW ✦

1. On average, how many Sundays per month are you in church?

0   1   2   3   4   5   Circle your goal for this year.

2. Which idea will most improve your personal worship this week?

Prepare my heart   Ignore distractions   Piggyback on prayers   Turn palms upward   Give sacrificially   Receive communion   Glory in the gospel

3. Write two words that describe how you can be filled with the Spirit:

_____   _____

4. In which ways do you normally interact with God's Word?

Hear it   Read it   Study it   Memorize it   Meditate it

5. In which of these five ways do you normally pray to God?

Praise   Thanksgiving   Confession   Petition   Intercession

6. Make this prayer your own as you worship your Lord right now:

"Here I am, Lord. I am all yours. I present my body to You. Take my life, a living sacrifice. May it be holy and acceptable to You. I fully submit to Christ as my Lord. I trust you with all my life.

By your Holy Spirit, give me the power to resist the pressures to be conformed to this world. Remove from my life all those things that displease You. Transform my life by the renewing of my mind. Remind me to daily be in Your Word. Use Your Word to remold my way of thinking, to reshape the way I feel, and to make me fully obedient to You.

Let me experience the confidence of knowing that my life is in the center of your will. Do with my life whatever You please. Glorify Yourself in me.

I realize my great need to be filled with Your Spirit today. I ask that You cleanse me. I confess my sins to You, and I commit myself to turn from that sin and to obey Your Word. I submit to your Holy Spirit and allow Him to take control of my entire life. I surrender completely to Your perfect will.

I admit that I am utterly dependent upon Your power to live my Christian life as it ought to be lived. Cleanse me, control me, fill me. Amen."

Section Four

WALK Until Christ Comes

Alittle boy once got his hand caught inside his mother's expensive vase where she stored her loose change. Mother was very upset. She applied soapsuds to his hand, then cooking oil, even shampoo. But nothing would work. Finally, she picked up a hammer and was ready to sacrifice the priceless vase in order to rescue her son's swollen hand. As she pulled back the hammer, ready to smash the family heirloom, the frightened boy cried out, "Would it help if I let go of the money?"

Can you identify with that problem? You'd like to get out of a mess you're in, but you don't want to let go of what you're holding on to of the world. You risk ruining what's truly valuable, all because you are too stubborn to let go of your sin. You must turn loose of your sin if you are to let God turn your life around. You must repent.

Is it a good thing when you turn away from a bad thing? Yes! Because that is true, "repentance" is a positive word. The word "repent" means to change your mind from what is false to embrace what is true, to change from living destructively to living constructively. In order to walk with God, you must repent of every area of your disobedience against God.

Wholly Holy

Christ calls you to prepare for His return by walking worthy of Him in holiness and purity of life. He wants to motivate you to lead a life of faithful service before Him (1

109

John 3:3; Matthew 25:14-30). He wants you to be so grateful for His amazing grace that you will obey Him with a thankful heart. The truest test of your love for Jesus is whether or not you will obey His Word. Jesus "tells it like it is" in John 14:15, "If you love me, you will obey what I command."

You can claim all day long that you love God, but you are just filling the air with religious talk until you are willing to obey what He has said.

God's purpose in giving you prophecy is not to satisfy your curiosity about the future. His purpose is to motivate you to holy living, so that you will live out the remainder of your days with a vital, positive anticipation of Christ's sudden return for you.

God's goal is not to fill your head full of fascinating ideas, but is to get inside your heart so that it has a dramatic effect on the way you live. God tells you what He will do in the future, not so that you will have a fuller head, but so that you will believe Him when He tells you that the glory of this world is not worth chasing after (1 John 2:15-17).

God tells you about future events, not so you will be filled with fear, but so that you will be filled with well-founded hope and unbounded joy. Prophecy is designed by God to motivate you to live a life of purity, holiness and faithful service for Him (1 John 3:3; Matthew 25:14-30).

The Apostle John often uses the term "walk" to describe the obedient Christian life. 1 John 1:7 instructs you to "walk in the light, as [Christ] is in the light." 1 John 2:6 asserts, "Whoever claims to live in him must walk as Jesus did." 2 John 6 adds, "And this is love: that we walk in obedience to his commands." 3 John 4 declares, "I have no greater joy than to hear that my children are walking in the truth." Let's focus on how Christ wants you to walk until He comes.

Seven Churches

In Revelation chapters 2 and 3, Christ pinpoints seven

areas of disobedience that tend to disrupt our walk with God. He uncovers seven specific areas where you may need to repent.

In the first century, the seven cities of Ephesus, Smyrna, Pergamum, Thyatira, Sardis, Philadelphia and Laodicea were situated on a circular road that networked them together. A postal worker delivering mail to these seven cities would follow this order on his route.

Christ wrote letters to these seven churches because their spiritual condition represented all Christians in all ages. What Christ says to them speaks to you, no matter what your country or your century. By listening carefully to what Christ praises and what He rebukes, and by subjecting yourself to the scrutiny of Christ's evaluation, you receive a very clear picture as to the kind of Christian He wants you to be during your last days on earth prior to the return of Christ.

In order to walk with God, every Christian needs to repent of the same seven particular sins that Christ pointed to in Revelation 2-3.

Get ready for God's bright spotlight - and sharp scalpel - to examine your heart.

I hold this against you: You have forsaken your first love.

◆ *Chapter 14* ◆

Repent of Forsaking
Your First Love

A re you ready for your first self-examination of your heart? Then climb up on the cardiologist's examination table and let's begin!

The first common sin that you may need to repent of is the sin of falling out of love with Jesus. The church in Ephesus was guilty of this sin. Jesus begins speaking to these Christians with words of praise in Revelation 2:2-3:

> I know your deeds, your hard work and your perseverance. I know that you cannot tolerate wicked men, that you have tested those who claim to be apostles but are not, and have found them false. You have persevered and have endured hardships for my name, and have not grown weary.

This church had four incredible strengths.[35] First, at the core of the Ephesian church was a busy and dynamic ministry. Hard-working believers were constantly serving Christ. There were no spectators here longing to be entertained. These were not lazy, lethargic members in "a spiritual country club." They were motivated to teach the Bible, witness for Christ, and feed the poor.

Second, this church would not "tolerate evil men." They set high moral standards. If a member slipped into sin, they would lovingly confront him and call him to repentance. With holy zeal, they disciplined those who continued to practice evil. They didn't look like saints on

---

[35]I wish to give much credit for the insights in this section to Steven Lawson's book *Final Call*, 78-85.

Sunday and act like aint's on Monday. They were serious about their walk with Christ.

Third, this church tested false apostles. It was a citadel of orthodoxy, a fortress for the faith. They did not run after every theological fad that came along. Their doctrine was well defined and well defended. They could smell a heretic a mile off. When they heard theological error, alarms went off and flares went up. False teachers were given a road map and sent on their way.

Fourth, despite growing opposition to Christ, this church was rock-solid. They wouldn't waver from their mission. They were not quitters. They were sturdy, determined disciples, faithfully working and witnessing and not growing weary of the truth they had received.

Up to this point, this church could claim a grade of A+. If you attended one of their church services, you would immediately sense you were with God's spiritual Marines: the few, the proud, the Ephesians. If you moved to Ephesus, you would want to join this church. It was steady, strict, steadfast and strong. They had all the right stuff. People were plugged in. Programs were bursting loose. The place was hopping! What could possibly be wrong with a church like this?

Plenty. They had everything but the main thing.

Abruptly, Jesus changes the tone of this letter. The Master puts His finger on the one glaring deficiency in this church that threatened to ruin everything else. He addresses a fatal flaw, a deadly sin so serious that it endangered the church's very existence. Jesus announces in Revelation 2:4, "Yet I hold this against you: You have forsaken your first love."

Does this rebuke send a bone-chilling tingle up your spine? What does it mean? It means that the more busy they became for Christ, the farther they drifted away from their original pure and simple love relationship with Christ.

Infatuating Feelings

What is first love? First love is that fervent, passionate, red-hot love of a new couple when they start courting seriously. Chemistry takes over. A mystical attraction occurs. Two hearts heat up and beat in sync. It is well described by the woman who wrote:

I climbed up the door, and I shut the stairs.
I said my shoes, and took off my prayers.
I shut off my bed, and climbed into the light.
And all because he kissed me tonight![36]

That is first love. When you see first love in a couple, it's so sweet, it's sickening. As soon as their swooning eyes meet, they run into each other's arms and kiss and don't care who is watching. It is obvious that their love relationship is the preeminent priority of their lives. But then, something happens along the way. Somewhere in the daily routines of marriage, the honeymoon ceases. The career takes off, the children come, the business expands, the activities increase and the stresses multiply. After several years, two people wake up complete strangers.

It was this kind of slow leak that left Ephesus flat emotionally. Their devoted love for Christ had not died; it had just cooled off on the back burner. Their ministry had become mechanical. Their relationship with Christ had become routine. Their hearts were no longer on fire. Somewhere in all their busyness, they lost their passion for Jesus. They had lots of activity for Christ, but little intimacy with Christ. They had full heads and busy feet, but their hearts had sprung a slow leak.

Imagine your husband or wife coming home and saying to you, "I don't love you anymore. But don't worry. Nothing will change. I'll still earn a living and help pay the bills. We'll stay together in the same house and I'll still

---

[36]This poem was composed by Faith A. Mills.

help parent our children. I just won't love you anymore."

Would that be good enough for you? No way. You would be devastated. Yet, so often, isn't that what we say to the Lord? "Jesus, I don't love You like I once did. But don't worry. I'll still come to church. I'll still serve You. I'll still witness for You. I'll even still tithe. I just don't love You as much anymore. I hope You will understand."

Is that OK with the Lord? No way! Why not? Because if we don't love Him with "first love," we disobey God's greatest commandment. It doesn't matter what else we obey, if we fail to keep the highest commandment, we have struck out! Leaving our first love is a serious sin.

How is it with you? Is your spiritual honeymoon over? Has your love for Jesus faded? Has your Christian life become humdrum and routine? If so, you have forsaken your first love. You haven't lost it completely. You're still a Christian. It's easy to still play church, to attend the right Bible study, to use the right lingo. You can fake it. But the more you do, the emptier you feel. There's a dull feeling deep inside. You have drifted away from your Lord.

How can you recapture your first love? Jesus specifies three steps to take in Revelation 2:5: "Remember the heights from which you have fallen! Repent, and do the things you did at first."

Remember

Step one is to remember. Do you remember that love you felt for Jesus when you first came to know him? Do you recall that wonderful sense of discovering that He loved you so much that He died in your place to free you from the penalty of your sins? You could hardly believe that you were really forgiven. Your sense of peace was overwhelming. You had eyes for no one but Him. You were head-over-heels in love with your Savior. Every time you opened the Word of God, it had something new to say to you. Whenever you prayed, all heaven seemed to open up to you. Wherever you went, you longed to tell people about Him. Jesus urges, remember what that was like. Replay that initial excitement. Refocus on those times when you were "fresh in love" with Jesus.

Repent

Step two is to repent. Repentance means to change your mind, to change the direction of your life. It means that you point your finger at whatever it is that you now love more than Christ. It may be your job, or a relationship, or your education, or your house or a new form of entertainment. It's anything or anyone that you are more excited about than you are about Christ. Acknowledge the fact that you have let this person or thing usurp first place in your heart and repent!

Humbly drop to your knees and confess it as spiritual adultery. Say, "Jesus, my heart has gradually grown distant from You. I've been far away from You because I've let [fill in the blank] get in between us. But Lord, I want to change. I want to turn my life around starting today. Right now, I'm rededicating my life to You. God, I want to regain a fresh passion for you in my life."

Return

Step three is to return. Jesus invites you to "do the things you did at first." Repeat the spiritual activities you once enjoyed at the beginning of your Christian life. Let go of those other things that have crowded Christ out of your life, those activities that seem more enticing, and return to the essential "basics" that feed your love for Christ.

Those "basics" are to spend much time in God's Word and in prayer. It is the Word of God that stimulates your hearts to love Christ and inflames your passion for Christ. It is prayer that gives you intimate fellowship with Him and keeps you fervent about your love for Him. Spend time in the Bible, both in personal devotions and in small group Bible study. Spend time in prayer, both privately, and with a small committed circle of Christian friends. Fan the flames of your first love.

In your comfortable complacency and breakneck busyness, have you given your heart to lesser things? If so, take deliberate steps to be alone with Christ. Make definite plans to recapture your first love. Remember when you first met Christ. Repent of your cold-heartedness. Humble yourself before Christ and admit where you have drifted. Tell Him you long to renew your passionate love for Him today.

◆ *Chapter 15* ◆

Repent of Your Fear of Suffering

How are you doing so far? Did that first exam hurt very much? May we now proceed to examine the second sin that you may need to repent of? It is the sin of being fearful of suffering pain or persecution for your faith in Christ.

To the church in Smyrna, God encourages Christians to commit themselves in advance to be faithful to Him, even to the point of enduring a martyr's death.

Smyrna was easily the most beautiful city in all of Asia Minor, a thriving seaport city nestled in a picturesque, natural setting. It was called "the Crown of Asia." Alexander the Great had determined to make Smyrna the model Greek city, and it had blossomed into a town of advanced culture and great wealth with a magnificent library.

This city was a major center of emperor worship. Every citizen was called upon to publicly worship and confess allegiance to Rome's ruler annually.

To this persecuted church, Jesus writes in Revelation 2:9-10:

> I know your afflictions and your poverty–yet you are rich! I know the slander of those who say they are Jews and are not, but are a synagogue of Satan. Do not be afraid of what you are about to suffer. I tell you, the devil will put some of you in prison to test you, and you will suffer persecution for ten days. Be faithful, even to the point of death, and I will give you the crown of life.

Jesus speaks only words of comfort to this church. No correction is needed, just encouragement. Why? It is because a persecuted church tends to be a pure church.

The name Smyrna means "myrrh," which was a fragrant spice used to make perfume. When the bark of the flowering myrrh tree was crushed, it releases a sweet aroma. Myrrh appropriately described this church because the more these believers were crushed by the world for their faith in Christ, the more the sweet aroma of their testimony was released. Their faithfulness to Christ in the face of mounting opposition gave off the fragrance of Christ throughout the entire region.

When Jesus says, "I know your afflictions," He is saying, "I know exactly what you're going through. I know because I've been there. I know what your tribulation feels like. I know what it is to be falsely accused, physically harmed and spit upon. I know what it is to be beaten, mocked, and suffer unjustly, and I highly value your commitment to Me."

These people who associated with Christ and who did not conform to culture were persecuted unmercifully. Christians' homes were confiscated because of their stand for Jesus Christ. Because they refused to worship Caesar as god, they lost jobs, civil rights, even their lives. The wicked Roman emperor Nero would tie Christians to the stake, cover them with pitch, then set them on fire, using them as living torches to light up his imperial gardens at night. Even today, in seventy-eight nations, a staggering one third of a million Christians are martyred for their faith each year.

This church at Smyrna was being crushed through persecution. These Christians faced continuous cruel and persistent hostility (2 Timothy 3:12).

Jesus speaks of five different levels of persecution they were suffering.

Government

First, they faced government persecution. "Afflictions" means being imprisoned by the Roman government. They were being crushed in an ironclad political vise grip that was squeezing out their life-blood. They were being snatched from their homes and taken to prison.

Economic

Second, they faced economic persecution. They were financially destitute. Even though Smyrna was one of the most prosperous cities of its day, and everyone else in Smyrna was prospering, these Christians were extremely poor and on the verge of starvation.

Religious

Third, they faced religious persecution. They were being slandered by a large Jewish community which was fanatically hostile against Christianity. Their reputations were being ruined. Christians were accused of being cannibals because they spoke of eating and drinking the body and blood of Christ. They were accused of being atheists because they refused to visit the pagan temples and worship the pagans' gods. They were accused of incest because they talked often about being members one of another and of loving one another as brothers and sisters. Every good thing they did became twisted and warped by slanderous lies.

Physical

Fourth, they faced physical persecution. They were thrown into ghastly Roman prisons where they were severely tortured (fingernails pulled off, hung by their thumbs for days, wrapped in animal skins in arenas for bulls to gore and to pitch around) then slung back onto the streets.

Satanic

Fifth, they faced satanic persecution. The devil was unleashing his hellish hatred against these believers by inciting unbelievers to be filled with extreme hatred toward them. But Jesus, in His mercy, promised to limit the intensity of their persecution to only "ten days."

You may cringe at descriptions of torture that seem so far away, barbaric and archaic. But the startling fact is, more Christians have been martyred for their faith in the Twentieth Century than in the previous nineteen centuries combined. In China, Christians in non-registered churches are imprisoned. In Pakistan, radical Muslims offer a bounty of $30,000 for killing a Christian. In North Korea, they have attempted to stamp out Christianity by requiring the worship of the nation's leaders. In Saudi Arabia, conversion to Christianity is a crime punishable by death. In Sudan, over one million Christians have been killed by Moslems and over three million have had their homes burned and property confiscated. Even in America, Christians are consistently portrayed in the movies as dangerous bigots and demented serial killers.

If you were being persecuted, you would not wander away from your trust in the Lord. You would cling tightly to Jesus' promises in the Scriptures every day. Why? It is because a persecuted church tends to be a purified church. The church in the Third World nations that are dominated by Islam or Eastern religions may be poor, but in their love for Christ, they are pure and strong.

Although Jesus does not rebuke this church, we are rebuked by our comparison to it. Are you fearful of being persecuted for Christ? If so, God says, "Repent!" Do not be fearful if persecution or suffering comes your way. If God allows it, permit God to use it to purify your faith in Him.

◆ Chapter 16 ◆

Repent of Your
Financial Materialism

This next one may hurt a bit. Bite down hard. Hold on tight to the table. The third sin you may need to repent of is materialism.

Christ addresses the issue of loving money more than God when He speaks to His church in Pergamum. He "nails" them in Revelation 2:14 because, "You have people there who hold to the teaching of Balaam."

What is "the teaching of Balaam"? It is that you should pursue money as your highest goal. In Numbers 25, Balaam is a "for profit prophet" who had been hired by Balak, the King of Moab, to curse Israel. He accepted pay to become a traitor to God's people.

Three times Balaam tried to curse Israel, but each time, God made words of blessing come out of his mouth instead. So Balaam devised an insidious plot that would force God to curse them. He instructed Balak to parade a bunch of beautiful, sensuous girls from Moab and Midian before the eyes of the young men of Israel to entice and lure them into sexual immorality. These young Israeli soldiers wilted under their seductive power and began to party with these pagan women. They ended up sleeping with them and worshiping their idols. As a result, God had to judge them for their disobedience by killing twenty-four thousand Israelite men.

The teaching of Balaam is to compromise with the world in order to make money and get rich.

This heresy is taught today under the name of

"prosperity theology." It's known as the "health and wealth" gospel, or the "name it, claim it" teaching. It feeds greed, arouses materialism, stimulates worldliness and pampers covetousness. It sidetracks Christians with self-indulgence, leading them to become preoccupied with their own monetary success.

Breaking Babylon

When Christ returns, He will destroy the economic and materialistic harlot of Babylon. What is the meaning of God's command in Revelation 18:4 to "Come out of her, my people, so that you will not share in her sins"? It means, stop wasting your wealth on selfish, excessive luxuries. Stop letting your mind be raped by sound bytes and spin doctors who flatter you to believe you are entitled to more. Stop serving Mammon, the god of money, instead of serving God.

The two things that characterize "harlot Babylon's" lifestyle are pride and luxury. She is known for her puffed up, self-glorifying pride and for her sensuous, luxurious living, parading her wealth for all to see.

That describes the United States almost too well. We want the whole world to love us and look up to us as the earth's leading nation, yet while we consume our wealth frivolously on entertainment and fun, half our planet goes to bed hungry every night.

God abhors materialism because it is a powerful form of both idolatry and adultery, the two sins that God says He hates the most.

Materialism is spiritual idolatry because it deceives you into thinking you are self-sufficient apart from God and blinds you to your own spiritual poverty. Materialism is spiritual adultery because it consumes all your time and attention with work and worry and causes you to be smothered by your own possessions. It takes time to hover over your things. Every item you add to your pile of possessions is one more thing to think about, talk about, pay interest on, clean, repair, display, rearrange, insure, worry about losing and replace when it breaks. The result is just like Jesus said in the parable of the soils in Matthew 13:22: "the worries of this life and the deceitfulness of wealth" choke you, making you unfruitful for God.

In Hosea 13:6, God laments about His people: "When I fed them, they were satisfied; when they were satisfied, they became proud; then they forgot me." This is a perfect description of many churchgoers in the United States. Forty percent of Americans go to church on Sunday, yet polls show that the lifestyle of the average born-again evangelical is no different than the lifestyle of a pagan. When it comes to statistics on divorce, premarital sex, use of alcohol, pornography, and levels of credit-card debt, church-going people are, on the average, not much different from their neighbors.

Have you swallowed the hook of materialism? Do you love the world more than you love God? Do you love your TV more than you love your Bible? Do you love your telephone and computer and ball games more than you love prayer? Do you love your money and investments more than you love your Lord? Have you gotten yourself so deeply in debt that you can easily convince yourself that it is impossible for you to tithe to God?

Costly Compromise

Pergamum pictures a church that compromises with the world's lure of profit. As a Christian living in an increasingly godless society, the pressures to compromise for money are tremendous. The real question is: Have you succumbed to them? Have you cheated, stolen or taken advantage when it comes to your own financial integrity? Have you justified, rationalized or compromised to make a buck? Has God brought something specific to mind? If so, repent!

We live in a post-Christian America. Never before has the church so desperately needed to be the church. To be the church, the sin of materialism must be dealt a decisive deathblow. The hope of America lies not in the White House, not in Wall Street, and not on Main Street, but in the pure church of Jesus Christ.

Stop flirting with the world. Refuse to succumb to "money hungry idolatry." Humble yourself before the Great Physician and accept His cure: open-heart surgery.

Jesus proclaims in Revelation 2:16, "Repent therefore! Otherwise, I will soon come to you and will fight against them with the sword of my mouth." The "sword" is the power of capital punishment, representing the power of the government to put criminals to death. Jesus can also use that sword like a scalpel to excise from your heart the spiritual cancer of materialism, if you repent.

Will you submit to His scalpel-like sword today?

◆ Chapter 17 ◆

Repent of Your
Toleration of Immorality

The fourth sin you may need to repent of is one that is epidemic in America. It is the sin of being too tolerant regarding sexual immorality.

In Revelation 2:19, Christ first praises the church in Thyatira for its good deeds, love, faith, service and perseverance. It was a growing church with a vital, youthful energy. It was an active and attractive church with some wonderful people. They had everything the church in Ephesus had, plus love.

But below the surface, something was rotten. The blazing eyes and the burning feet of Jesus go into action to reveal some dirt on this church in Revelation 2:20-23:

> I have this against you: You tolerate that woman Jezebel, who calls herself a prophetess. By her teaching she misleads my servants into sexual immorality and the eating of food sacrificed to idols. I have given her time to repent of her immorality, but she is unwilling. So I will cast her on a bed of suffering, and I will make those who commit adultery with her suffer intensely, unless they repent of her ways. I will strike her children dead. Then all the churches will know that I am he who searches hearts and minds, and I will repay each of you according to your deeds.

This is a scathing rebuke. The bottom line is, this church was strong on love, but weak on truth.[37] Out of love,

---

[37]Ephesus was just the opposite. They had truth, but no love. Christians often are polarized in one or the other direction. Either they will have full heads and empty hearts, or full hearts and empty heads. Either polarization is deadly. God demands both love and truth. Paul instructs us in Ephesians 4:15 to "speak the truth in love."

they tolerated the sin of Jezebel, but in so doing, they sacrificed the truth.

Liberal Lies

The sin of Jezebel comprises the sin of sexual immorality in all its various forms:

*Some Christians look at pornography and attend sexually explicit movies. That is wrong.

*Many believers, fearful of appearing old-fashioned, refuse to speak out against pre-marital fornication among teenagers and the practice of "living together" before marriage. That is wrong.

*Some denominations sanction the ordination of practicing homosexuals into pastoral ministry. That is wrong.

*Some churches condone divorce and remarriage without any biblical grounds. That is wrong.

*Others quickly reinstate adulterous pastors back into their pulpits without lengthy, disciplined accountability and restoration. That is wrong.

*Many approve of killing unborn infants in the womb. That is wrong.

*Most churches fail to discipline church members who are sexually unfaithful to their spouses. That is wrong.

*Some tolerate pornography in the private lives of their leadership. That is wrong.

All these practices arise from the teaching of Jezebel.

Throughout the years, your Bible hasn't changed one bit. God still commands, "You shall not commit adultery" (Exodus 20:14); "Flee immorality" (1 Corinthians 6:18); "Let the marriage bed be undefiled" (Hebrews 13:4); and "Do not let immorality or any impurity . . . even be named among you" (Ephesians 5:3). Because God is holy, sexual promiscuity has a payday someday. Play with fire and you'll get burned. Sow to the flesh, and you'll reap a whirlwind of misery.

Personal Purity

How do you personally apply these commands from God? Singles, are you keeping yourselves sexually pure until your wedding day? Are you guarding your virginity with all your might? Men, are you renting sexually explicit videos? Are you reading pornographic magazines or looking at porn on the Internet? Are you having an affair? Are you even thinking about having an affair? Women, are you fantasizing about someone else? Are you watching "soaps" or reading sensual "harlequin" fiction? Are you flirting with disaster? Even one drop of poison will pollute the entire glass of water. Jesus warns, "Don't tolerate any kind of sexual sin."

Thyatira is the "too-tolerant" church. Today, the watchword that best describes the mind-set of the American church is the word tolerance. Most Americans worship at the shrine of tolerance. In the shaping of public opinion and the forging of national policy, our society praises the broadmindedness that claims that any and all values, if sincerely held, are equally valid.

In our culture, there are no more absolutes. The only absolute is that there are no absolutes. We are told to tolerate everything except intolerance. George Gallup, America's pollster, has revealed that sixty-seven percent of Americans believe that there is no such thing as absolute truth. Two thirds of Americans believe that what is right and wrong varies from situation to situation. People think, "It may be wrong for me, but right for you." What this means is that modern man has both feet planted firmly in midair.

As a nation, our moral senses have been tragically neutered. We have undergone a moral lobotomy. The sin that used to slink down the back alley now struts down Main Street and into the Oval Office. Like ancient Israel, we have become a people who have forgotten how to blush. Nothing shocks us anymore. Tragically, out of a desire to be tolerant of diversity, we have become desensitized toward sin and have opened the floodgates to wickedness.

Is that true in your own life? Have you adopted a "too tolerant" attitude towards sexual sin? God will execute His judgment upon all who refuse to repent. The church of Thyatira needed to be disciplined by Christ because it had not disciplined itself. Though it was the smallest church of the seven churches in Revelation, Christ's message of rebuke to it was the longest of all seven.

The philosophy of seduction is eating our culture alive. It's ripping out the very heart of our society. The church today needs courageous leaders who will execute church discipline on church members, leaders who will vigilantly uphold the moral-conscience issues of our day regarding the sins of abortion, pornography, pre-marital sex and homosexuality.

Will you be that kind of Christian? Will you encourage your church leaders to not compromise on moral truths? God expects you to live out your Christianity with integrity, love and authenticity before the eyes of a watching world.

Christ's blazing eyes see everything in your life. Nothing is hidden. Allow the double-edged word of God to cut out of your life or church any cancerous growth that may be growing there. Repent in humility before the God who sees it all. Turn your eyes and your mind from enticing lures to sexual immorality. Resist the insidious appeals to grab a glimpse of flesh, as if the most important thing in life is to just experience more sensual pleasure.

Choose to be holy and obey your wonderful Lord.

◆ *Chapter 18* ◆

Repent of Your Spiritual Apathy

Are you still fully awake and alert? That's important, because the fifth sin you may need to repent of involves spiritual apathy.

Jesus speaks to the church in Sardis and urges it to wake up from their spiritual slumber. Revelation 3:1 states, "I know your deeds; you have a reputation of being alive, but you are dead."

Jesus, the Great Physician, having just completed His examination of this church, pronounces it dead. Despite rumors that this church was still alive, it was not. Their sanctuary was a morgue with a steeple. The building was open, services were held as usual, but there was no life of God pulsating through it. It was a congregation of corpses.

Is your own spiritual life like that, dead, dormant and dull? Maybe you once were excited about your faith in Christ, but now your heart is lifeless. Your walk with Christ has dried up, withered on the vine with no more life left in it.

That describes the church at Sardis. There was no pulse, no heartbeat. They were phony and hypocritical, surviving only on a hollow reputation. It was a church full of lethargic zombies, some saved, some unsaved. This church was on the verge of extinction. They were simply cruising on past glory, living in the "good old days."

Dead Churches Stink

Dead worship services are like a funeral service. The preaching is like an old heater with a burned-out coil: the blower is still working, but the heat is gone. Congregational singing sounds like two calves dying in a hailstorm.

Cobwebs are spun in the baptistry. The congregational motto is the seven last words of the church, which are, "We've never done it that way before."

There are only two things you can do with a dead church. Either you must resuscitate it with vigorous CPR, or you must bury it. How do you resuscitate a dead church? It requires genuine Spirit-sent revival. Only the Holy Spirit has the power to revive a dead church.

Jesus provides the five steps that are required in that process. He gives us five commands that are, in the Greek, sharp words, like a quick slap in the face, designed to stimulate a person to immediate action.

Five Steps to Revival

Step one is directed to the unsaved in verse 2 where Jesus commands, "Wake up!" If you are spiritually dying or dead, your first need is to wake up[38] from your corpse-like condition.

Have you ever fallen asleep while driving on the freeway? It's scary, isn't it? After a second of sleep, when you wake up, you receive the biggest adrenalin rush of your life. You become instantly alert to make the immediate correction. This is the kind of urgency that Jesus is talking about here. He is shaking them from their sleepy stupor and shouting, "You are in a dangerous and desperate situation! Come out of your spiritual hibernation! Wake up, NOW!"

This command to wake up implies that some people in the church of Sardis were not yet saved. They needed to stop their fairy-world illusion about being Christians and really become Christians. They needed a sharp slap in the

---

[38]The town of Sardis was known as a sleepy, careless city. It was built on a high mountain plateau 1500 feet above the valley floor. People there felt protected and secure from military attack. The citizens thought they were invincible against invading armies. However, twice in its history it had been conquered by surprise attacks. Each time it had failed to guard its walls adequately at night. Both times, a few brave soldiers climbed up the sides of the ravine in the dead of the night and overthrew the city. Because of this lack of alertness, Sardis gained the reputation of being a city that was not awake.

face to awaken them, a cold splash of water, a stiff sniff of ammonia, to motivate them to radically reverse their current direction.

Are you a church member in good standing? That is no guarantee that you are saved. Is it possible that to your horror, you might one day hear Jesus say to you, "Depart from me; I never knew you"? If so, snap out of your daydreaming and do serious business with God.[39]

On the other hand, to those who were already saved, Jesus states in verse 2, "Strengthen what remains and is about to die, for I have not found your deeds complete in the sight of my God."

Step two towards revival involves strengthening what remains. Go back to the basics of your spiritual life by taking time for Bible study, prayer, worship and fellowship. Stir up the cool embers and fan them back into flames.

Jesus gives the next three steps to revival in rapid-fire order in Revelation 3:3 when He urges, "Remember, therefore, what you have received and heard; obey it, and repent."

Step three is to remember where you've been. Remember your rich spiritual heritage in Christ. Remember how you were saved. Remember how God's grace reached down and redeemed you.

Step four is to obey God. This means, submit completely to the authority of God's Word. Quit making excuses and start keeping all His commandments. Where God has put a period, don't put a question mark. Selective obedience is no obedience at all; it's merely convenience.

Step five is to repent. If you're saved, make an immediate decision to leave your sin, turn around and come running back to Christ with all your heart. Confess your sin of spiritual lethargy. Do an immediate about-face. Make a

---

[39]To help you become certain of your salvation, pause now to read Appendix A on page 217.

quick and decisive U-turn in your thinking and behavior. Why? Because repentance means to "change your mind."

Have you been guilty of spiritual deadness and apathy?

If so, wake up. Strengthen what remains, remember what you used to do when you were growing spiritually, obey your God and repent!

◆ *Chapter 19* ◆

Repent of Being Ashamed
of Christ's Name

We are getting close to being done soon. Can you hang in there a bit longer? The sixth sin you may need to repent of is the sin of being ashamed and embarrassed of being identified with the name of Jesus Christ.

The Lord praises the church in Philadelphia in Revelation 3:8, "I know that you have little strength, yet you have kept my word and have not denied my name."

This church was surrounded by a bunch of hostile, unsaved Jews, and when it came to witnessing, this little band of believers did not buckle under to worldly pressure. Wherever they went, the name of Jesus was always on their lips. Boldly, they witnessed for Him at every opportunity. Other people knew they belonged to Jesus Christ. They named the Name without shame and embarrassment. That is why Christ says to them in Revelation 3:8, "See, I have placed before you an open door that no one can shut." This speaks of an open door for witnessing about Christ, a door that you must be willing to walk through to share the good news with a lost soul.

Many Christians are far too concerned about being embarrassed by being identified with Christ. Why? It is very unlikely you will ever be called upon to be a martyr in this country prior to the rapture. Of what are you so afraid? A tiny bit of humiliation? Being laughed at? Being called horrible names like "old fashioned" or "fanatic" or "fundamentalist"? Not being invited to the company

Christmas party? Are those things important enough to keep you from opening your mouth to tell your friends about the best news they will ever hear?

God's truth is worth telling, regardless of the risk. God wants you to choose to be a witness to the people He has placed within your private world. He wants you to willingly identify yourself with Christ by wearing His name, being unashamed to verbally let others around us know that you are a Christian. Why? Because witnessing to the truth has the power to produce life.

1 Peter 4:16 urges, "if you suffer as a Christian, do not be ashamed, but praise God that you bear that name."

Are you "not ashamed" of the name of Christ? If so, you won't act awkward if someone finds you reading your Bible or praying over lunch. You won't wimp out when you have an opportunity to take a stand for pro-life moral issues. You won't be intimidated to stay silent when your science teacher asks, "No one in this class still believes in the myth of creation in Genesis, do they?" Instead, you will stand alone as a Christian who will not shrink back from being identified with the name of Christ, no matter what the cost.

Are you ashamed to bow your head in a public restaurant to give thanks for your food? Are you ashamed to invite your neighbor to church because you fear he might ridicule, revile and reject you for doing so? Do you shy away from using the name of "Jesus Christ" properly around other people? You should try it. Say the name "Jesus Christ" out loud, and in public, in a non-swearing way. You may be surprised at the odd reaction you receive. But, so what? Why should you be ashamed of Jesus' name?

If you struggle with this, repent of your self-conscious embarrassment. Choose to be like the Philadelphians who did not deny Christ's name.

◆ Chapter 20 ◆

Repent of Your
Spiritual Lukewarmness

Do you like warm soda? How about cool coffee? Neither one sounds very appetizing, does it? God doesn't like them either. That's why the seventh sin you may need to repent of is the sin of spiritual "lukewarmness."

This sin is so subtle, and so common, you may have difficulty believing it applies to you.

Christ writes to the church that lived in Laodicea in Revelation 3:15-16:

> I know your deeds, that you are neither cold nor hot. I wish you were either one or the other! So, because you are lukewarm—neither hot nor cold—I am about to spit you out of my mouth.

The church at Sardis was a cold church, and the church at Philadelphia was a hot church, but this church in Laodicea was neither hot nor cold. It was lukewarm, air temperature, bland, boring, not refreshing at all.

Archaeologists have discovered an interesting fact about this city that explains this for us. Nineteen hundred years ago, the city of Laodicea had a major problem. It did not have a good local water supply. Its drinking water had to be brought in from nearby towns through aqueducts from two outside sources. One aqueduct brought water six miles from Colossae, where the water was very cold and refreshing and good for drinking. Another aqueduct brought water from Hierapolis, which was famous for its underground hot springs, where people would go to sit in the water for medicinal purposes to bring comfort to their aching bodies.

Two Paths to Putrid

The problem was, by the time the cold water from Colossae arrived in Laodicea, it was no longer cool and refreshing to drink. It had become lukewarm. In the same way, by the time the hot water of Hierapolis arrived in Laodicea, it had cooled off along the way. It had adapted to air temperature and was also lukewarm.

How does water become lukewarm? The cool water can warm up and the hot water can cool off. In a similar manner, people become spiritually lukewarm in two different ways.

Some people begin spiritually ice-cold toward Christ, but then warm up to lukewarm. These people attend church, and because of it, others assume that they are Christians. But they have never been born again. They are still unsaved, even though they have gradually adapted to the warm environment in the church. They are lukewarm, and not saved.

Other people begin burning red-hot for Christ, but then cool off and adapt to the environment around them. They lose their fervency for Christ. They also are room temperature, but are saved.

Test Your Temperature

Which category might you place yourself in spiritually? With respect to your personal relationship with Jesus Christ, would you say that you are cold, hot or lukewarm?

To be cold means to be spiritually indifferent or apathetic. A cold person has zero interest in the things of God. He is frozen in unbelief. He openly and boldly rejects the gospel, even to the point of being openly hostile. Such a person is clearly lost, unsaved, and separated from God. Jesus said in Matthew 24:12, "Because of the increase of wickedness, the love of most will grow cold." Such hearts are icy toward the gospel of Christ. They are unresponsive, hardened, frozen, ice-cold.

To be hot means to be spiritually on fire for God. A hot person is fired up about spiritual things. He is inflamed with spiritual fervency for Christ, consumed with a red-hot passion and a burning zeal for His Lord. After His resurrection, Jesus appeared to two disciples on the road to Emmaus. After sharing intimate fellowship with Him, they said in Luke 24:32, "Were not our hearts burning within us while He was speaking to us . . . explaining the Scriptures to us?" Their hearts were on fire with a glowing love for Him. They were definitely hot.

To be lukewarm means to be half and half, half cold, half hot. This person is halfhearted toward Christ, a fence-straddler, not willing to commit one way or the other. He has one foot in the world and one foot in the church. Lukewarmness is a matter of yawning in Christ's face. It is the sin of being bored with Jesus, as if Jesus Christ was no big deal. A lukewarm person has enough religion to bring him to church, yet not enough relationship with Christ to truly change his life.

Have you pegged yourself yet? In which category are you? Are you lukewarm?

Shockingly, Jesus says that's the worse category of all. He would actually prefer that you be cold rather than lukewarm. He'd prefer that you were all-out against Him—then at least you'd know where you stood. The worst option is to ride the fence.

Are you possibly a person who is trusting in your church membership or in your good moral life to bring you to heaven? Are you lukewarm and not yet truly saved? Or, are you possibly a saved person who is lukewarm? Either way, Jesus says the same thing: shape up or ship out. Why? It is because lukewarm Christians have a devastatingly negative effect on unbelievers.

He is the worst advertisement for Christianity there is. As a hypocrite, he is a negative witness.

If you are determined to be a sour-puss person, don't tell others you are a Christian. It would be better for you to claim to be an atheist so that you would help out God's kingdom in reverse!

Lukewarm Believers

According to Jesus, a lukewarm churchgoer is nauseating and repulsive. He makes Jesus sick. Jesus says, ". . . because you are lukewarm . . . I am about to spit you out of my mouth."

Have you ever taken a big gulp out of a Pepsi bottle after it had been left open in the sunshine for a few days? Yuck! It's awful. Lukewarm pop doesn't quench your thirst at all. The same is true with lukewarm coffee. Hot coffee is good, and iced coffee is fine, but lukewarm coffee is nauseating. It's good for nothing but to dump it down the sink.

When Jesus sees lukewarm churchgoers, it makes Him want to spit. It gives Him nausea. He wants to throw up. This is strong language. In fact, it's crude language. It means literally, to vomit, barf, puke, regurgitate.

Does that shock you? Good. Jesus wants you to be repulsed by what repulses Him. He has real feelings, you know. Jesus Christ is not some impassioned accountant in heaven. He is not simply making marks in His divine ledger, running the universe in a cold, calculated way. He is a person with deep emotions, passionate zeal and a loving heart. He longs to have a personal, intimate relationship with you, which is why indifference is so unacceptably repulsive to Him.

What is the cause of this indifference toward God? Why are so many Christians lukewarm?

Jesus exposes the problem in Revelation 3:17 where He quotes their own words:

> You say, 'I am rich; I have acquired wealth and do not need a thing.' But you do not realize that you are wretched, pitiful, poor, blind and naked.

Self-Image Adjustment

These people are absorbed with the things of the world, climbing the social ladder, advancing their career, getting ahead in the world and sporting the latest fashion styles. They are buying the latest toys with a "Shop-til-you-drop" attitude of smug self-sufficiency. Their thought is, "We don't need anything because we have big bank accounts. Why pray? God has already blessed us."

But Jesus' assessment of them was 180 degrees different than their estimate of themselves. They thought they were O.K., but Jesus said they were K.O.'d.

Jesus remarks, "You think you're pretty hot stuff, but in reality, you're wretched. You think you're happy, but behind your plastic smiles, you're pitiful and miserable. You think you've gotten ahead in the world financially, but in real wealth, you're broke! You think you can see life clearly, but spiritually, you're as blind as a bat. You think you're well-dressed, but in terms of real clothing, you're disgustingly naked!"

In His assessment of these people, Jesus highlights three things: their gold, their clothing and their eyesight. That's because Laodicea was well known in the ancient world for three things: its banking industry, its clothing industry and its medical school.

Laodicea was a prosperous banking center. Its citizens were used to having lots of financial counselors give them advice about how to invest their money wisely. As a wealthy financial center, great sums of gold, silver and Roman currency were kept on deposit there.

Laodicea had a flourishing textile industry that was famous for its fine, glossy, black wool. The local factories were famous for weaving this black wool into expensive garments. Consequently, they were a fashion-conscious town, always up on all the latest styles.

Laodicea also was a famous medical center. It's physicians developed a well-known eye salve that helped cure eye diseases. This is why these people claimed they could see so well.

Laodicea was a Chase Manhattan Bank, Nordstrom and Mayo Clinic all rolled into one. These facts make Jesus' words to them pertinent and pointed. With their banks, they thought they were rich, but spiritually, they were poor. With their wool clothing, they thought they were decked out in fashion, but spiritually, they were naked. With their eye salve, they thought they could see perfectly, but spiritually, they were blind.

What a huge difference there is between "what you think you are" and "what you really are." The problem is, Jesus declares, lukewarm Christians "do not know" their true condition. Like an alcoholic who claims he has his drinking problem under control, they live in denial.

Christ's challenge to this church mentions these same three areas again in verse 18:

> I counsel you to buy from me gold refined in the fire, so you can become rich; and white clothes to wear, so you can cover your shameful nakedness; and salve to put on your eyes, so you can see.

The financial counselor who claims now is a good time to reassess your investments and readjust your stock portfolio is Jesus. The shopping consultant who advises that you need to buy a new set of fashionable winter coats and sweaters is Jesus. The physician who reminds you that this is a good time to make an appointment at your optometrist to have your eyes checked is Jesus.

He is the true and faithful witness. This isn't just a Dear Abby column. This is not a horoscope, not a health and beauty-tip, not an investment counselor giving some advice. This is Jesus speaking to you.

The key to this verse is the three little words "buy from me." Jesus has all you really need to function: Pure gold, white clothing and eye salve. He alone is the source of all good things. These things can be "bought" from Him without money (Isaiah 55:1). He is willing to give away all

He has, but to receive it, you must come directly to Him.

Jesus Is All You Need

First, He offers us "gold refined in the fire." This pictures a genuine faith in God, which is more precious than gold (1 Peter 1:7). Genuine faith, knowing Jesus, is what makes us truly rich.

Second, He offers us "white clothes to wear." This pictures our need for righteousness before God. Every person is born morally naked before God, for "all have sinned" before God (Romans 3:23). God sees you in your nakedness. He offers to cover you up with the perfect righteousness of Christ. White clothes stand for being washed "as white as snow" in the blood of the Lamb.

Third, He offers us spiritual eye salve. This is a picture of the Holy Spirit, who enables you to see life as it really is. The anointing of the Holy Spirit is what opens blind eyes to understand the truth of God. You need the illumination of the Holy Spirit to open your spiritual eyes.

Jesus shows you how to receive these things from Him in the next two verses. He shows the way out of lukewarmness. In Revelation 3:19, He speaks to lukewarm saved people who have cooled down. He says, "Those whom I love I rebuke and discipline. So be earnest, and repent."

This verse is addressed to Christians because God only disciplines His own children (Hebrews 12:5-11). As a father, I don't discipline my neighbor's children. I only discipline my own children. Jesus is saying, "Because I love you as part of My own family, I will discipline you."

Jesus tells lukewarm Christians to be "earnest" or "zealous" in repentance. That word means to be on fire, to be hot. He's saying, "Get on fire for Me again. Make your heart hot toward Me again." If your passion for God has cooled off, Jesus says He wants you to turn up the flame.

Where Do You Stand?

As a Christian, God commands that you repent of your sins. He wants you to continually and consciously live in dependence on His grace and mercy each day. Christ doesn't just want to be your Savior. He also wants to be your Sovereign–the Lord of your life–without a lot of static from you. He seriously desires genuine purity and holiness in your walk with Him.

Which of these seven church sins apply to your personal life right now? Will you deal with that issue seriously before God? Will you carve out time to perhaps fast and pray over it, or read a book about it, or make an appointment with an accountability partner to talk about it in the open?

If you do, it will make you more ready for the rapture, for you will be prepared to meet Jesus with confidence. You will find yourself more eagerly anticipating His coming than you were before.

Lukewarm Unbelievers

In Revelation 3:20, Jesus speaks to unsaved lukewarm church attenders who have warmed up to Christianity, even though they are not yet genuine believers. They are involved in church, but are not yet involved personally with Christ. They are lukewarm, lost church attenders. To these, He says, "Here I am! I stand at the door and knock. If anyone hears my voice and opens the door, I will come in and eat with him, and he with me."

What does it mean? The door represents the entrance into your heart. At that door, Jesus stands knocking, seeking entrance. He's been there for a long time. He is patiently knocking. He is gently pounding on your heart– not so hard as to hurt you, but firm enough and persistent enough to remind you He's there.

Jesus is big, strong and powerful. He is God. He could easily knock that door down. But He is a gentleman. He waits to be invited in. That's your human responsibility.

You must personally respond to His call by faith and open your heart to receive Jesus as your Savior. As an act of your will, you must personally invite Christ to come live within you. As John 1:12 states, ". . . to all who received Him, to those who believed in His name, he gave the right to become children of God."

Receiving Christ as Savior requires repentant faith. You receive Christ by grace, through trusting Him. There are no good works involved in the process. It involves you admitting to God that you are a sinner who needs a Savior, believing in your heart that Jesus Christ died for you on the cross, in your place, and that He arose from the dead.

When Christ enters your life, He "dines" with you. Eating a meal is a picture of close and intimate fellowship with another person, visiting, talking, listening, encouraging. Having a personal relationship with Christ means you can pour out your heart to Him and tell Him anything you want. You can share with Him your deepest concerns and greatest needs, twenty-four hours a day, seven days a week. Once He comes in, He'll never abandon you. He comes to stay.

Will You Answer?

Revelation 3:20 pictures the simplest explanation in the whole Bible of how you can become a Christian. Perhaps you realize you may not yet be a true Christian, and that this is a decision that God is calling on you to make right now. Jesus desires to have a personal relationship with you.

Do you sense that Christ is outside your life, knocking at the door of your heart, wanting to come in? Do you sense the knocking of Christ? Do you want Him to come in?

If so, you must open the door. He will not force Himself upon you. He offers salvation to you as a free gift, and it's up to you to receive His offer. You must invite Him in. You must say to Him, "Come in, Lord Jesus. I receive you into my life. I want You to be my God and Savior today."

Will you, at last, surrender to Him?

God loves you. He wants to introduce you to a plan for living that is far superior to the plan you've been running with lately. He wishes to take away all your guilt and give you a fresh start with a clear conscience and a new purpose for living. He desires that you experience true freedom from the behaviors and habits that bind you and control your life. He offers you a full, abundant, fulfilling and meaningful life. Jesus alone can do that. You can't find that kind of life without Him.

Jesus stands and knocks, waiting to come in. He doesn't invite you to a religious lifestyle, or to an organization, or to a system of doctrine, or to a set of disciplines. He invites you to enter into a personal relationship with Him. If that is a decision you want to make, say to Him, "Come on in."

Jesus clearly announces in John 14:6, "I am the way, the truth, and the life. No one comes to the Father except through me." Ephesians 2:8-9 affirms:

For it is by grace you have been saved, through faith— and this not from yourselves, it is the gift of God—not by works, so that no one can boast.

Will you choose to believe what God's Word says to you?

Go ahead. Open the front door to your heart by saying this prayer to Him:

Dear God, Thank you for creating me and for continuing to love me, even when I've ignored you and gone my own way. I realize I need you in my life. I believe that Jesus Christ died on the cross for me, in my place, and then rose from the dead. On the basis of what You did for me, I ask you to forgive me for all my sins. I trust Jesus to be my personal Savior. I now receive Him as my Savior and God. Make me a new person inside. I accept your free gift of salvation through faith. As much as I know how, I want to follow you from now on. Please help me to grow as a Christian. In Jesus' name, Amen.

Did you pray that prayer? If you meant it, you are now a Christian. Christianity is not a religion; it is a relationship with Christ. Salvation is not just moving you out of hell and into heaven. It involves "moving" Christ out of heaven and into you.

If God were to ask you, "Why should I let you into My heaven," what would you say? I hope you could honestly say to God: "I don't deserve heaven, but you promised that if I trust in Christ's death and resurrection, depending on Your grace, You would forgive my sin and give me the gift of eternal life. By faith, I'm depending on You to keep Your promise to me."

If that's your answer, the Bible says that you have been born again (John 3:3; Titus 3:5). Welcome to the worldwide family of God! Trust God completely to now guide you into life's greatest adventure!

◆ PERSONAL APPLICATIONAL REVIEW ◆

1. How intense is your "first love" relationship with Jesus Christ?
I love Him   I'm slipping a bit   I've slid a lot   I am backslidden
What will you do about it? _____ *(Hint: Remember ... Repent ... Return)*

2. Are you afraid of suffering for Christ?   Yes   No   Maybe
Which kind of persecution do you fear most? _____
Are you willing to allow God to use it to purify you?   Yes   No   Maybe

3. Have you compromised with materialism?   Yes   No   Some
How? Dishonest business   Greed   Prosperity theology   Other
What do you plan to do about it? _____

4. Have you condoned or tolerated sexual immorality?   Yes   No   Some
How? Sex outside marriage   Pornography   Bad movies   Other
What do you plan to do about it? _____

5. To what degree is your spiritual life dead, dormant and dull?
None   A little   Some   A fair amount   A lot   Totally   What would it
look like in your life if you "woke up" from spiritual slumber?

6. Are you embarrassed of Christ's name?   Yes   No   Some
Check which activities you will to do: Pray over my meals in public
Read my Bible at lunch time   Invite a neighbor to church   Witness

7. What temperature is your love for Jesus Christ?
I'm still hot and in love   I love Him a lot   I am loyal to Him
I'm a bit lukewarm   I'm very lukewarm   Frankly, I'm rather cold
I have warmed-up from being cold   I have cooled-off from being hot

8. Will you communicate daily with God in the Bible (2 Timothy 3:16-17) and prayer (Philippians 4:6), attend a Bible-teaching church (Hebrews 10:25), be discipled by a mature Christian (2 Timothy 2:2) and share your faith with others (Colossians 4:5-6)?   Yes   No   Maybe

Section Five

WORK Until Christ Comes

The story is told of a sailor who was shipwrecked on a South Sea island. He was seized by the natives, carried shoulder-high to a rude throne and proclaimed king. He learned that according to their custom, the king ruled for a year. The idea appealed to the sailor until he wondered what had happened to all the previous kings. He learned that when a king's reign ended, he was banished to a lonely island to starve to death.

Knowing he was king for one year only, this sailor began issuing orders. Carpenters were to make boats. Farmers were to go ahead to this island and plant crops. Builders were to erect a home. When his reign finished, he was exiled, not to a barren isle, but to a paradise of plenty.

You are like that sailor king. Your time on earth is short, but during this brief window, you do have opportunity to work hard and send provisions on ahead. God invites you to store up for yourself treasures in heaven that you will then be able to enjoy for billions of trillions of years.

How can you build up that heavenly bank account? By voluntarily, sacrificially giving of your time, treasure and talent to advance the kingdom of Jesus Christ while you still have the chance.

Titus 2:13-14 says that "while we wait for the blessed hope—the glorious appearing of our great God and Savior, Jesus Christ," God wants us to be "eager to do what is good." Titus 3:8 also instructs us to "be careful to devote themselves to doing what is good."

Untaught Truth

If you are from a conservative church, you maybe haven't heard much about the doctrine of good works. Somewhere along the way of emphasizing the fact that you are not saved by your works, you may have picked up the idea that "works" is a dirty word in God's sight. That's not true! While God condemns the idea of performing works to earn salvation or to impress others, God enthusiastically commends you for performing good works for the right reasons.

Contrary to what so many people erroneously believe, everyone will not be equal in heaven. Not everybody who is saved will receive an equal reward. If they did, then God would end up validating and condoning all those lives spent in selfishness, laziness, indifference and apathy. It does not make sense that a Christian who spends his life supporting missionaries and feeding the hungry and sharing the gospel and praying for widows, would end up with no more than the one who grabbed his "fire escape from hell" and then lived any way he pleased after that.

No. Galatians 6:7 warns, "Do not be deceived: God cannot be mocked. A man reaps what he sows." In harmony with that principle, some will be rewarded more than others. Some will receive nothing. Some will be given charge over ten cities, some will be given one city, and others, none at all (Luke 19:12-27).

God invites you to prepare for the rapture by doing good works that will result in eternal rewards at the judgment seat of Christ (1 Corinthians 3:11-15; 2 Corinthians 5:10). God does not want you to be so earthly minded that you are no heavenly good. He expects you to consciously live each day in light of the eternal consequences that God will give to you, because the kind of heaven you experience will be determined by Christ's judgment on your works.

Ecclesiastes 12:14 promises that "God will bring every

deed into judgment." Romans 14:10, 12 adds, "we will all stand before God's judgment seat" and "each one of us will give an account of himself to God." Revelation 2-3 teaches that Christ is continually watching and evaluating you for your works. He is keeping score and grading you. He states in Revelation 2:23, "I am he who searches hearts and minds, and I will repay each of you according to your deeds."

The Scriptures teach that a significant part of Christ's reasons for rewarding you will have to do with how faithfully you have worked at using your time, your treasure and your talent in serving Him while you await His return.

The next three chapters will illustrate this practical concept in crisp detail.

"We are God's workmanship,
created in Christ Jesus to do good
works, which God prepared in
advance for us to do."

◆ Chapter 21 ◆

Use Your Time in Good Works

E either death, or the rapture, will be the final deadline that will determine what kind of heaven you will have. A basketball game is over at the final buzzer. No shots taken after the buzzer count. Likewise, once this life is over, your eternal status will be fixed forever. If you have been disobedient, you will have no second chances to live rightly. If you pass into the next life with a grade of "D-," you cannot improve it to an "A" later on.

Ephesians 2:10 affirms that "we are God's workmanship, created in Christ Jesus to do good works, which God prepared in advance for us to do." God created you to do good works, and He has a whole lifetime of good works waiting for you to complete. He wants you to fulfill various roles of service that He had planned out for you even before you were born.

God will reward you, or not, based on whether or not you used your time wisely to do the good works that He has entrusted to you throughout your life. He does not want you to "take it easy" and retire early from the work of the Lord. He doesn't want you to try to get by with as little as you can, but rather He wants you to abound in as much as you can for Him.

Needy Neighbors

Our world is an incredibly needy place. In Nigeria, I've seen people who are lame, hobbling around on rough, crude crutches, begging for alms with an old rusty bowl. In New York City, I've had to step over ragged homeless drunks who were curled up asleep on main city streets. In

153

Venezuela, I've been inside homes built out of corn-stalk huts.

Most people on earth are very poor.

Have you ever had to deal with a request for help from a transient? As a pastor, I've had to handle many such calls. It is difficult to listen to bad-luck stories from a man needing gas money to get to a new job, or from a mom who says her children are hungry and in need of medicine. There are two reasons why I find it so hard. One, I never know if the story is true or if it has been spun by a professional bum who is sponging up handouts so he can buy another bottle of booze. Two, if I discern that the story is likely true, I feel guilty if I refuse to get involved.

One passage that convicts me is 1 John 3:17-18:

> If anyone has material possessions and sees his brother in need but has no pity on him, how can the love of God be in him? Dear children, let us not love with words or tongue but with actions and in truth.

Another one is James 2:14-17:

> What good is it, my brothers, if a man claims to have faith but has no deeds? Can such faith save him? Suppose a brother or sister is without clothes and daily food. If one of you says to him, "Go, I wish you well; keep warm and well fed," but does nothing about his physical needs, what good is it? In the same way, faith by itself, if it is not accompanied by action, is dead.

My back-door excuse for not getting involved is that both passages speak not about helping all poor people, but just needy brothers and sisters in Christ. That makes me feel much better, because after all, our church has a Deacon's Fund to handle that. Right?

Then I think of Galatians 6:10, "as we have opportunity, let us do good to all people, especially to those who belong to the family of believers."

Yes, as Christians, we are to take care of our spiritual family first, but God also calls us to do good "to all people" in order to show them His love, as well.

When was the last time you chose to say "No" to an obvious need? How did that decision make you feel? Pretty rotten, huh? There is no easy way out. It's uncomfortable to be confronted with a need that could cost you dearly in time, money or effort, if you were to do anything about it.

This problem is not new to our 21st Century. Jesus, in John 12:8, said, "The poor you will always have with you." Despite all the anti-poverty strategies and economic policies that have been tried throughout the centuries, Jesus' prophecy continues to hold true.

Good Sam

In Luke 10, Jesus told a story that brings us face-to-face with that difficult and bothersome question of "What kind of good works does God realistically expect me to do?" It's the story of the Good Samaritan, the man who loved his neighbor as himself.

In Jesus' day, the term "Good Samaritan" was a contradiction in terms. To a Jew, there was no such thing as a "good" Samaritan. Samaritans were a hated half-breed, half Jew and half Gentile, despised and disowned by both Jews and Gentiles alike.

Part of Jesus' purpose in telling this story was to shock His listeners out of their racial prejudice and bigotry, so that they might come to see all people as neighbors whom we need to love and serve regardless of their race, color or creed.

Jesus tells of a man who was bushwhacked by robbers who brutally beat him up and stripped him of everything he possessed, including his clothing. It is a pathetic portrait of a man with deep genuine needs, lying naked, bleeding, filthy, half-dead in the dirt. This man is in sharp pain, dizzy and faint, afraid to even try to move, and listening, listening for footsteps of someone who might possibly be coming by who would be able to help.

After a long time of waiting in pain, his ears perk up because he hears footsteps coming. It is a priest. But he quickly crosses to the other side of the street. Because he is in a hurry to go do his religious duty, he turns his back on a man who is agonizing in pain.

The mangled man hears other footsteps approaching. It is a Levite, an active worker in the temple, a servant of God. He also hurries away. Though he is above average in wealth and could have easily met the man's need, he refuses to respond at all. His lack of compassion displays his cold heart.

This poor beaten man continues to lie there helpless in his hurt until finally, clop-clop-clop, on a donkey, comes a man with a compassionate heart. Luke 10:32-35 explains:

> But a Samaritan, as he traveled, came where the man was; and when he saw him, he took pity on him. He went to him and bandaged his wounds, pouring on oil and wine. Then he put the man on his own donkey, took him to an inn and took care of him. The next he took out two silver coins and gave them to the innkeeper. 'Look after him,' he said, 'and when I return, I will reimburse you for any extra expense you may have.'

Jesus points to this man as a true neighbor at work. He is willing to go out of his way to stop and help a stranger of another race. He is willing to kneel down and get his hands and knees all full of little scratchy sticks and stones and dirt. He is willing to use up his wine to cleanse the man's wounds, to use up his oil to sooth the pain, and to use his own clean clothes to bandage up his bloody wounds.

By stopping, the Samaritan was perhaps endangering his own life, for it was not safe for him to linger in a robber-infested area. But despite that risk, this man decided to spend his time, his energy, and his emotion, to help a fellow human being in need. He got bloodstains on his own clothes, and then placed his own fortune at the disposal of this total stranger, so that his immediate physical needs would be met.

What is Jesus' definition of a neighbor? It is anyone whom God brings across my path who has a need that I am able to meet. My neighbor is anyone who has a need I see, whom I have the ability to help through the investment of my time in good works for him.

Who is your neighbor? God wants you to love that person by demonstrating compassion for his need and show him love through personal involvement in good works. That might mean stopping at the scene of a car accident, or caring for someone who is dying of cancer, or visiting someone in a nursing home. It means being willing to face an un-beautiful situation and emotionally cross over to the other side of the road in order to help relieve someone else's pain.

Jesus says in verse 37, "Go and do likewise." Let the indwelling Christ love that person through you. Be controlled by the Holy Spirit rather than by a busy schedule and a tight wallet.

Good works come in all shapes and sizes. A five year old can share a smile and a kind word. A ten year old can give a toy away. A 15 year old can donate his time to mow a lawn. A 25 year old can run some errands or chop some wood for someone who's having a personal energy crisis. A 30 year old can fix a meal for someone who has been hospitalized. A 50 year old can offer a spare room for a college student at low rent. A 70 year old can offer some frozen meat and some cans of pears from her shelf. You can't do everything, but you can do something.

Composing Your Obituary

Alfred Nobel was a Swedish chemist who made his fortune by inventing dynamite and other powerful explosives that were purchased by governments to produce weapons for war. When Alfred's brother died, one newspaper accidentally printed Alfred's obituary instead. It described him as a man who became rich by enabling people to kill each other in unprecedented quantities.

Shaken by this assessment of his life's work, Nobel resolved to use his fortune to do something good for mankind by rewarding those accomplishments that benefited humanity. So he established a large trust fund for what is now known around the world as the Nobel Peace Prize.

Alfred Nobel had a rare opportunity: to look at the assessment of his life at its end, and then to still be alive to have the opportunity to change that assessment. You can do that right now. Through the Scriptures, you can read your own obituary from heaven's point of view. You can then determine to use the rest of your life to edit that obituary to become what you really want it to be.

Your Time Is Limited

Once the rapture occurs, what you are, and what you have done for Christ, will be fixed for all eternity. There will be no more second chances for you to make different choices. The effect of the rapture will be similar to dying, in that all your life's choices will be set, fixed and unchangeable.

At the judgment seat of Christ, you will have to give an account of your life to God. This judgment will determine your place and status and position in heaven for all eternity. If, as a Christian, you make the choice to live your life in full obedience to Him, you will be eternally glad you did. But what if you choose to live this life as though it was the only one there is, living only to satisfy your own pursuit of pleasure and comfort in the here and now? I guarantee that you will be kicking yourself for the next trillion years, because you will have missed out on all of God's extra eternal rewards that He had hoped to be able to give to you.

God's Word speaks of Christ's judgment seat with great seriousness. This will not be a mere meaningless formality of "going through the motions" that you hurry through before getting on to the real business of enjoying heavenly bliss. Rather, the Bible presents this as a monumental event in which eternal consequences are put into effect forever.

If you fail to invest time in good works, will it really

matter? Yes. The loss of rewards that you otherwise could have enjoyed in heaven will be the consequence for the selfish choices that you have made here on earth (Colossians 3:25). On the other hand, Revelation 14:13 promises that if you labor for the Lord, your "deeds will follow" you into heaven.

How are you using your time? How can you invest it in a God-pleasing "good work" this week?

"Where your treasure is, there your heart will be also."

◆ Chapter 22 ◆

Use Your Treasure
in Generous Giving

The second major yardstick that God will use to determine your eternal rewards at the judgment seat of Christ is how you use your treasure on earth. In fact, a potential major obstacle to your receiving significant eternal rewards could be your lack of obedience to God's Word in the area of finances.

This chapter is longer than normal because the Bible has so much to say about how we give.

Jesus emphasizes the importance of our giving habits in Matthew 6:19-21:

Do not store up for yourselves treasures on earth, where moth and rust destroy, and where thieves break in and steal. But store up for yourselves treasures in heaven, where moth and rust do not destroy, and where thieves do not break in and steal. For where your treasure is, there your heart will be also.

When you give money to God, you really don't lose anything. You actually are making an investment in the building up of God's kingdom now that will pay back vast eternal riches to you as dividends later on. God invites you to invest in an eternal retirement account that is just as real and far more solid than any IRA, Keogh or annuity fund you can find here on earth.

You can't take it with you, but you can send it on ahead.

Genuine Discipleship

Are you afraid of being generous in your giving? The New Testament focuses a lot of attention on this one spiritual discipline because it makes or breaks a life of genuine discipleship.

How much treasure has God placed in your lap? Are you being faithful to distribute some of it to others in obedience to His will? Are you furthering His kingdom purposes through the faithful use of the financial blessings that He has given to you?

In Philippians 4:17, Paul clarifies, "Not that I am looking for a gift, but I am looking for what may be credited to your account." Your consistency in giving is rewarded by God. He credits it to your heavenly bank account. God adds rewards to your eternal treasure chest. When you give, there is actually a greater benefit in it for you than there is for the recipient of the gift.

Why should you sacrificially give money instead of enjoying it all for yourself? Because contrary to popular belief, there will not be total equality in heaven. You will be given a unique amount of rewards, calculated in part based on your degree of financial generosity on earth.

That's why Paul declares in 1 Timothy 6:17-19:

> Command those who are rich in this present world not to be arrogant nor to put their hope in wealth, which is so uncertain, but to put their hope in God, who richly provides us with everything for your enjoyment. Command them to be good, to be rich in good deeds, and to be generous and willing to share. In this way they will lay up treasure for themselves as a firm foundation for the coming age, so that they may take hold of the life that is truly life.

Compared to the rest of the world, you are rich. There is so much money in the United States that our federal IRS code is twice as long as the Bible. There are twice as many lawyers and accountants to interpret it as there are pastors. Regardless of what you may think, you are wealthy.

Affluenza Attack

All this incredible wealth has infected our society with an epidemic called "affluenza." Affluenza is a slow, insidious virus that takes over your brain and causes you to sacrifice your commitments to God and to your family on an imaginary altar of financial success. Affluenza distorts your sense of values and priorities to the point that you end up serving the god of possessions, power and privilege, the god that Jesus calls "Mammon." Affluenza causes you to care more about the false hope of winning the lottery than you do about the spiritual needs of the people around you who are headed for hell.

All this ignores the fact that he who dies with the most toys is still dead.

The only antidote for affluenza is for you to give the first-fruits of your treasure to God. This regular discipline forcibly reminds you that you are not the owner of what you earn or inherit; God is. He is the One who has given you the ability to gain that wealth. He owns it all. So that you don't forget that fact, He asks you to give back to Him a tenth (or more) of what He has given to you.

In Luke 12:15, Jesus warns, "Watch out! Be on your guard against all kinds of greed; a man's life does not consist in the abundance of his possessions." In other words, the quality of your life is not enhanced by adding more things to your list of assets. If you believe the lie, "If only I had that, then I'd be happy," you'll never be happy.

The act of giving is the only drain plug that God has provided to keep a check on your greed. God is not interested in your money as much as He is in your maturity. What you give to the Lord is a clear reflection of where your heart is toward Jesus Christ. The way you spend your money is the evidence of where your treasure truly lies.

Show me your checkbook, and I can write your biography, for it reveals who you are.

Luke 12:21 adds that anyone "who stores up things for

himself but is not rich toward God" is a fool. When God blesses you abundantly, He expects you to be willing to give away some of the extra rather than stockpile it and hoard it for yourself. God expects you to earn, spend, give and save your money in a God-centered way, not in a self-centered way.

Jesus' point is not that materialism is wrong, but that it is stupid. You may be a genius entrepreneur in the business world, but if you fail to take into consideration the fact that you may not have much time left to use all that money for yourself, you're a fool. You have never yet seen a hearse pulling a U-Haul. That's because when you die, you leave it all behind.

Write Your Will

Practically speaking, you need to write your will. Decide how much of your assets your family will really need after you are gone. If they don't need all that you have, or if all your wealth might become a spiritual stumbling block to them, perhaps you could give a large chunk of it away to support world missions or other ministries instead.

Leaving an inheritance to your children is wonderful. Proverb 13:22 says, "A good man leaves an inheritance for his children's children." Proverb 19:14 affirms that, "Houses and wealth are inherited from parents." God does not want you to leave your children destitute.

However, it would not be wise to leave them a huge inheritance until they have proven themselves to be faithful stewards before the Lord.[40]

---

[40]It would be foolish and immoral to leave money to children who have not yet demonstrated that they are morally capable of handling it well. If you suspect your children might waste and squander it, perhaps you should entrust a portion of your estate to your adult children now, while you are still alive, as a test to see what they will do with it. This will help you to determine how much of your estate should instead be left to churches, parachurch ministries and missions organizations that you feel confident will serve kingdom purposes until the Lord returns.

Seven out of ten Americans die without a will, largely due to procrastination. To die without a will that designates at least some assets to God's work would be as foolish as the rich farmer in Luke 12. On the other hand, a wise steward might choose to designate ten to fifty percent of his estate to support world evangelization and missions. Or, he may choose to "do his giving while he's living so he's knowing where it is going." Either way, he will be "rich toward God."

If you truly believe the Lord may likely return before you die, I suggest that you include in your will a "rapture clause." It might state that in the event that you and all of your named Christian relatives decease or vanish within a week's time, none of your assets shall be distributed to any government or supranational authority. Instead, they shall be given in full to any individual who meets three criteria: he is Jewish, he lives in Israel, and he is actively and publicly proclaiming that Jesus Christ is the true Messiah and Savior. Direct that this person may use these funds as he sees fit to spread the gospel of salvation through Christ throughout the world.

By such a clause, you will act in faith to attempt to keep your funds away from the antichrist and put them into the hands of one of the 144,000 witnesses.

Invest in Heavenly Currency . . .

In Luke 12:33-34, Jesus invites you to:

Provide purses for yourselves that will not wear out, a treasure in heaven that will not be exhausted, where no thief comes near and no moth destroys. For where your treasure is, there your heart will be also.

Instead of continually filling stock portfolios that will someday crash, start piling up wealth in your heavenly bank account that will last forever. That treasure will never be exhausted, stolen or wasted. Storing up treasure in heaven is a whole lot smarter than hoarding treasure on earth. As missionary martyr Jim Elliot stated, "He is no fool who gives what he cannot keep to gain what he cannot lose." Self-serving greed is foolish. Sacrificial generosity is wise.

Christ offers you the incredible opportunity to trade earthly goods and currency for eternal rewards. By putting your money and possessions in His treasury, you can provide yourself with eternal rewards beyond your wildest comprehension.

You can actually trade temporal possessions that you cannot keep anyway to gain eternal possessions that you cannot lose.

. . . Not Confederate Cash

Imagine for a moment that you are alive at the very end of the Civil War. You are living in the South, but your home is really in the North. While in the South, you have accumulated a good deal of Confederate currency. You also know for a fact that the North is going to win the war and that the end could come at any time.

The question is: What will you do with all of your Confederate money?

If you were smart, you would trade in your Confederate currency for U.S. currency, the only money that will have value once the war is over. You would keep only enough Confederate currency to meet your basic needs for that short period of time until the war is over and that temporary money becomes worthless.[41]

As a believer, you know that the currency of this world will become worthless to you, either at your death or at the rapture, both of which are imminent. This knowledge should radically affect your investment strategy. To continue to accumulate vast earthly treasures in the face of that inevitable future would be as foolish as stockpiling

---

[41] Randy Alcorn, *Money, Possessions and Eternity* (Wheaton, IL: Tyndale House, 1989), 128-9.

Confederate money despite your awareness of its eventual worthlessness.

God says if you are wise, you will convert your funds from earth's currency to heaven's currency. Your choice is to either hang on to weak wealth on earth, or to invest it in strong wealth in heaven that will still be working for you a few million years from now.

In Luke 16:10-15, Jesus speaks these sobering words:

Whoever can be trusted with very little can be trusted with much, and whoever is dishonest with very little will also be dishonest with much. So if you have not been trustworthy in handling worldly wealth, who will trust you with true riches? And if you have not been trustworthy with someone else's property, who will give you property of your own? No servant can serve two masters. Either he will hate the one and love the other, or he will be devoted to the one and despise the other. You cannot serve both God and Money.

The Pharisees, who loved money, heard all this and were sneering at Jesus. He said to them, 'You are the ones who justify yourselves in the eyes of men, but God knows your hearts. What is highly valued among men [possessions, power and privilege] is detestable in God's sight.'

Everything you possess is God's. He owns it all. As a Christian, you are a manager of God's money that He has entrusted to you temporarily. You are to manage it for Him wisely and faithfully, in accordance with His clear instructions. God never wants you to imagine that it is all yours. If you start using it all as though it were yours, it is embezzlement. God is watching to see how trustworthy you will be as a caretaker of God's assets that He has entrusted to you while you are on earth.

When you give money away, it is a freeing, liberating release. At last you can feel that the grip of Mammon's stranglehold on your life is broken, and your loyalty to your true Lord is secure. Giving is an adventure in trust, and it results in being liberated from anxiety, greed and fear.

In your own giving to God, do you abound with excuses? Do you say to yourself, "I have too many bills to pay; I can't afford to give. The cost of living is too high. Perhaps when the kids are grown, I can give more"? Perhaps you mistake the high cost of living for the cost of living high.

Like it or not, your habit of giving is a clear indicator of your spiritual condition. It is the thermometer that tracks the temperature of your heart.

Inheriting A Fortune?

Baby Boomers and Busters tend to consume more and save less, buy more and give less, than the Depression / World War II generation that preceded them. Economists predict that over a short span of twenty years, eight trillion dollars in wealth will transfer to the Baby Boom generation alone. The largest movement of inherited wealth in all of world history is in the process of occurring right now, flooding the stock market with new dollars.

What do you plan to do when your inheritance comes? Will you pour it all into the stock market? Will you consume it selfishly? Or will you use a portion of it to fuel the spread of the gospel around the world before Christ returns? Busters who have the American Dream handed to them on a silver platter will be wise to use their vast wealth for the glory of God.

Rich Young You

In Mark 10, a wealthy entrepreneur walked sadly away from Jesus because he was unwilling to liquidate his assets for the cause of the Kingdom. Jesus had asked him to perform such an outrageous act in order to force this man to come face to face with his own sin.

By exposing his failure to keep the tenth commandment, "You shall not covet," Jesus put His finger on this man's greed and compelled him to admit that gold was his god.

The aftermath to the story of the "rich young ruler" is very instructive. As Peter watched this wealthy "Buster" hop into his red Ferrari and race back to his comfortable mansion on Upper Crust Ridge with its tennis courts, saunas and servant girls, Peter tried to assess the fair market value of his discipleship. He said to the Lord, "We have left everything to follow you!" (Mark 10:28). Peter was indirectly asking his heavenly stockbroker for a computer printout of his eternal retirement assets. He wanted to know, "What will I get out of all my sacrifice?"

Jesus took the time to reassure His disciples that their sacrifices for the kingdom of God will be generously repaid. Listen to Mark 10:29-30:

'I tell you the truth,' Jesus replied, 'no one who has left home or brothers or sisters or mother or father or children or fields for me and the gospel will fail to receive a hundred times as much in this present age (homes, brothers, sisters, mothers, children and fields–and with them, persecution) and in the age to come, eternal life.'

Jesus makes it clear that God will not be a debtor to anyone. He has promised that whatever you voluntarily give up for Him, He will one day reimburse you ten thousand percent for your investment of faith and sacrifice for Him. God will reward you a hundred-fold in heaven for everything you give toward the advancement of His kingdom here on earth. No matter how much you shovel out to God, God will always shovel even more back to you because God has the bigger shovel! Someday, God will generously repay you for the faith you displayed in giving up some of the temporal pleasures you could have enjoyed for yourself, for the sake of advancing the gospel around your community and around the world.

Stewardship For Dummies

How much eternal treasure have you accumulated in heaven? How much stock have you bought in the eternal Dow Jones? Maybe you or your company have paid into a retirement program or pension plan that will help care for your needs ten, twenty or thirty years from now. That's fine; it's good stewardship to plan ahead for that time when you can no longer work so long and hard.

But how much have you personally invested in view of the next fifty thousand years? How about in view of the next billion trillion years?

Eternity lasts a long time. A wise Christian will plan ahead for it by doing as Jesus so clearly tells you to do by sending some treasure on ahead. How can you do that? By being a faithful steward now through consistent, open-handed giving to meet the needs of God's gospel and of God's people while you still have the chance.

Generational Glory

If you are part of the generation that will be leaving some of this vast wealth behind to your descendants, make sure that some of your estate will be used for God's glory. Include your church, or a trusted mission board, in your will or living trust. Even if you have limited resources now, you can generously support and extend the ministry of the gospel long after your life is over through wise stewardship of your stocks, bonds, real estate and insurance proceeds.

Jesus asks you to make a total one hundred percent commitment to Him. Are you willing to give up everything you hold dear, if need be, in order to wholeheartedly and unreservedly follow Him? Are you willing to step down from the throne of your life and let Him take charge of every area of your life, including the control of your wealth?

In view of the short time you have left on earth before Christ returns, radical stewardship commitment is needed to financially fuel the final push to evangelize the world before the sand in God's hourglass runs out. The fields are ripe for harvest. Don't "play it safe" anymore. Don't wrap your wealth in the napkin of "caution" and "discretion" and bury it in the ground. Choose to live more recklessly and more strategically at the same time by taking a risk that shows your trust in the sure promises of God.

In Luke 21:1-4, Jesus makes an object lesson of a poor widow who acted recklessly with her money:

> As he looked up, Jesus saw the rich putting their gifts into the temple treasury. He also saw a poor widow put in two very small copper coins. 'I tell you the truth,' he said, 'this poor widow has put in more than all the others. All these people gave their gifts out of their wealth; but she out of her poverty put in all she had to live on.'

Obviously, Jesus loves it when you honor Him with generous giving, because it proves that you truly trust Him to meet your needs. Just keep in mind that the amount you give to God is not nearly as important as your attitude. God measures your attitude not by how much you give, but by how much you insist on keeping for yourself. From God's point of view, giving a high percentage of a little means more than giving a low percentage of a lot.

Giving With Gusto

Statistics gathered about the giving habits of Americans reveal that people with less income normally give a higher percentage of their income than do people with a large income. That is why, when you get to heaven, you will find that a lot of people who were poor on earth will be very rich in heaven, and a lot of folks who were rich on earth will be quite poor in heaven.

That's what Jesus meant when He explained that many who are first now will be last then, and many who are last now will be first then (Matthew 19:30).

In heaven, God doesn't keep track of how many thousands of dollars you give. Instead, He keeps track of the attitude of your heart that leads you to be sacrificial in your generosity. He looks at the percentage of what you kept for yourself. He watches what you choose to give up for yourself in order to demonstrate your trust in Him.

2 Corinthians 8:12 says clearly, "if the willingness is there, the gift is acceptable according to what one has, not

according to what he does not have."

In Luke 14:33, Jesus says, "any of you who does not give up everything he has cannot be my disciple." This command to "give up everything" speaks of surrendering your entire life to kingdom purposes, dedicating everything you have to be available, if needed, to further the gospel. Jesus will probably not ask you to liquidate all your possessions, give away all the money, and pull up stakes to become a traveling missionary. But He does ask you to totally eliminate any selfish hoarding of your resources. He does forbid you to embezzle kingdom assets for your own personal self-indulgence.

C. T. Studd was a rich and famous English athlete who made a radical choice. He sold his entire estate, gave the money away and went to the mission field to serve Christ. He reasoned, "If Jesus Christ be God and died for me, then no sacrifice can be too great for me to make for Him." He is the same man who penned these famous words:

Only one life, 'twill soon be past,

Only what's done for Christ will last.

Jesus wants you to be generous, not greedy, with the money that He has temporarily entrusted to you to manage for Him on the earth. He expects you to regularly examine your own heart for the cancer of greed. He seeks to cut out of your heart any selfish attitude toward money that will keep you from accumulating true treasure in heaven.

When you give, do not succumb to manipulative methods or gimmicks that seek to extract money out of you against your will. Don't ever give in to high pressure arm-twisting for pledges. In one church, the pastor asked for those who would contribute an extra $100 to the choir fund to please stand, so the alert organist began playing a lively rendition of "The Star Spangled Banner," with astounding results! Remember that the only kind of giving that is worth anything in eternity is that which flows from a heart that genuinely loves and trusts God.

Ultimately, giving is not God's way of raising money; it's His way of raising children.

How are you using your treasure?

Are you investing it in generous giving for eternal impact?

One day in heaven, when everything now secret will be shouted from the rooftops, will Jesus Christ expose you for your self-serving greed, or will He exalt you for your sacrificial generosity?

The pen that will write that chapter is in your own hand.

"I press on toward the goal to win the prize for which God has called me heavenward in Christ Jesus."

◆ Chapter 23 ◆

Use Your Talent
in Obedient Perseverance

God's rewards at the judgment seat of Christ will be based on how wisely you invest not only your time and treasure, but also your talent for Christ while here on earth. God wants you to be able to accumulate abundant eternal rewards through your faithful, persistent service for Him.

Jesus says to us in Luke 12:48:

From everyone who has been given much, much will be demanded; and from the one who has been entrusted with much, much more will be asked.

Some of your rewards in heaven will be determined by how well you persevere in obediently using the talents that God has given to you.

Paul challenges you with his example of perseverance in Philippians 3:12-14:

Not that I have already obtained all this, or have already been made perfect, but I press on to take hold of that for which Christ Jesus took hold of me. Brothers, I do not consider myself yet to have taken hold of it. But one thing I do: Forgetting what is behind and straining toward what is ahead, I press on toward the goal to win the prize for which God has called me heavenward in Christ Jesus.

Paul declares, "I have not yet tackled and taken possession of that goal for which Christ tackled me. I have not arrived at sinlessness. I am not yet perfectly conformed to Christ's character. In fact, I know I never will be until I see Him face to face. The driving motivation of my life here on earth is to get as close to that goal as I possibly can. I want my heartbeat to be in sync with the heartbeat of God. I'm heading toward that goal with all that I'm worth."

In this fragmented world that tempts you to be always off chasing a million and one disjointed pursuits, this single-minded determination of Paul's life is an attractive and inviting path. Paul's life did not consist of "these forty things I dabble in," but "this one thing I do!"

Paul experienced the freedom of the simple, uncomplicated life because he had his life purpose whittled down to one point, and it was this: knowing Christ better so that he could become more like Him. Paul had a one-track mind. This one compelling "must" unified his life. It gave him a single-minded zeal, a dogged determination to accomplish the one most important goal in all of life.

Focus on the Bull's-Eye

In order to hit the bull's-eye of the one central target of his life, Paul says he had to "forget those things which are behind." You, too, need a "holy disregard" for the past. You need to leave behind that heavy burden you've been carrying around as a result of that big mistake you made a long time ago. You need to forget about that bitterness you've harbored over having been painfully wronged. You need to give up being paralyzed by that certain past sin that weighs you down with so much guilt that makes you even doubt you can be forgiven. You need to release that grudge that has been eating away at your heart and chaining you to the past.

By faith, let it go. Don't mull over it any more. Obliterate it from your mind.

As you look to the future, where do you know God wants you to go in your Christian life? What are the things that lie ahead for you that are worth reaching for? Visualize what your life could be like if you left the past in the past and let God completely have His way with you. Don't be satisfied to sit and sour and stagnate at your current plateau of spiritual growth. Get ready to grow!

What specific spiritual goals do you believe God has for you?

Does your list include a consistent daily worship time with devotional Bible reading and prayer? Does it include developing your boldness and ability in sharing the gospel with unbelievers? Does it include squaring away your personal finances so that you can have confidence that God is pleased with your management of all the things He has loaned to you? Does it include your commitment to an intensive Bible study or discipleship course so the Bible can become more of an open book for you? Does it include developing close, transparent friendships with a few fellow believers that will survive through thick and thin? Does it include preparing yourself to serve the Lord as an elder, a deacon, a Sunday School teacher or a missionary?

Whatever it is for you, 1 Corinthians 15:58 exhorts you:

Therefore, my dear brothers, stand firm. Let nothing move you. Always give yourselves fully to the work of the Lord, because you know that your labor in the Lord is not in vain.

Stand Steadfast

To stand firm, to be "steadfast and immovable," means that you remain firmly settled, staying rocklike, motionless, with respect to your commitment to serve Christ. It means that you say "No" to the world. It means that you not be fickle, scatterbrained and erratic in your commitments to God, shifting back and forth between trusting God and not trusting Him. It means that you stick close to what you know is right, persevering to the end.

A teenage boy had decided to quit high school, saying he was just fed up with it all. His father was trying to convince him to stay with it. "Son," he said, "you just can't quit. All the people who are remembered in history didn't quit. Abe Lincoln, he didn't quit. Thomas Edison, he didn't quit. Douglas MacArthur, he didn't quit. Think about Elmo

McCringle ..." "Who?" the son burst in, "Who in the world is Elmo McCringle?" "See," the father replied, "you don't remember him. That's because he quit!"

God asks you to be persistent in your work for Him. He wants you to stay busy serving Him and invest all of your energies into obeying His will. He wants you to always give yourself fully to the work of the Lord, because you know that your labor in the Lord is not in vain. God wants perseverance to shine through you.

> Two frogs fell into a can of cream,
> or so I've heard it told.
> The sides of the can were shiny and steep,
> the cream was deep and cold.
>
> "Oh, what's the use?" croaked number one,
> "Tis fate, no help's around.
> Good-bye, my friend! Good-bye, sad world!"
> And weeping still, he drowned.
>
> But number two, of sterner stuff,
> dog-paddled in surprise.
> The while he wiped his creamy face,
> and dried his creamy eyes.
>
> "I'll swim awhile at least," he said,
> or so I've heard he said;
> "It really wouldn't help the world,
> if one more frog were dead."
>
> An hour or two he kicked and swam,
> not once he stopped to mutter,
> but kicked and kicked and swam and kicked,
> then hopped out, via butter![42]

---

[42] Author unknown.

Are you willing to work at having that kind of perseverance when it comes to trusting God's promises of eternal rewards? Are you willing to intensify your commitment to Christ, to live for Him "all the way"?

Exceed Expectations

To give yourself fully to God, to "abound" in the work of the Lord, means to exceed the requirements, to overflow and overdo yourself when it comes to saying "Yes" to God. It means to give your best efforts to the Lord, and live as if each day might be your last. It means realizing that "working for the Lord" is a necessary and essential part of fulfilling God's will for your life.

Leisure and relaxation are two modern idols to which God does not want you to bow down. Don't say, "I've served my time, I've done my part; now let others do the work." When it comes to your service within the church and your witness to the world, you are never done. You always need to abound, to give yourself fully to serve God and to obey His will.

Have you ever felt as though your labor for the Lord is meaningless or futile or unrewarding? Have you ever wondered whether it's really worth all the sacrifices you have to make to live for Christ and serve Him? The secret to staying motivated is in believing that your labor in the Lord is not in vain. It's not for nothing. Your efforts for God are never wasted because your future eternal rewards are very real. What keeps you going? It is in knowing that you will never regret your decision to live totally for Him. It is your certain hope of knowing that when the battle is over, you will win!

Think back to what it was like for our soldiers in World War II during those dark times when they weren't too sure if our side was going to win. It is very hard to keep up a high level of morale and motivation among troops who expect to lose a war. But, once they became convinced that they were definitely on the winning side, they could fight with renewed stamina, vitality and intensity.

After the bombing of Hiroshima, our troops had a tremendous boost of confidence. Although the battles were not all done, they knew the war was won. They had no doubt but that they were on the winning side.

The same thing is true of you as a Christian. You are in a war, a war against Satan, sin and death. Although your battles are not done, you know your war is won, because Jesus Christ, your General and Commander in Chief, has won it for you on two fronts: the cross and the empty tomb. Your side has already won! Based on what Christ has done, you can be absolutely certain that you will rise from the dead and your labors on earth will be rewarded.

With that confident hope, most of your fears of death and failure will be dispelled. That gives you an incredible amount of confidence and optimism when it comes to living your Christian life, for you know the day is coming when you will behold Him face to face, and then, you will share in His glory.

Christ expects you to live in full obedience to Him. Jesus Christ is not a passive, lenient, grandfather figure who ignores your misbehavior and pampers your spoiled selfishness. No. He is a holy judge whom slackers should fear. He is the One who calls you to discipline yourself for godly obedience and who warns you of loss of eternal rewards if you don't.

2 Peter 3:14 states, "So then, dear friends, since you are looking forward to this, make every effort to be found spotless, blameless and at peace with him."

To you, is this a positive incentive, or a scary thought?

How are you using your talents? Are you investing it in obedient perseverance?

It's Your Eternity

In light of the fact that your eternal rewards are conditional, what will you decide to do with your time, your treasure and your talents, over the last few years of your life on earth? Will you use them in a way that will result in great benefit to you that will last throughout the many trillions of years of your life in heaven? What part of your time will you invest in the lives of people? What part of your treasure will you freely give away now, knowing that God will multiply its value a hundred times "on the other side"? What part of your talent will you donate when it comes to serving the needs of God's people in His church?

The fact is, the answers you give to these questions will in large part determine the quality of your works that will survive that final fire at the judgment seat of Christ.

Eternity is a long time, and eternal rewards are worth accumulating. You are but one heartbeat away from seeing your Lord face to face at the judgment seat of Christ. At that time, all the hidden motives of your heart will be revealed. All that you have done for your own glory will be burned up; all that you have done for the Lord's glory will receive a reward. If you really believe that heaven will last forever, you need to prepare for it now, while you still can.

Here is what you need to do. Make yourself available to serve the Lord any way He wants you to. Let Him be the One who steers your life. Re-surrender your whole life to Him. Make Him your top priority in the use of your time, treasure and talent.

Make the choice to invest all that you are and have today in light of that coming Day that will last forever.

To help yourself walk along that path, please take a moment to complete the next Personal Applicational Review with relentless integrity.

✦ PERSONAL APPLICATIONAL REVIEW ✦

1. If you died or were raptured tonight, how many rewards would you expect? Nothing   Very few   A moderate amount   By grace, many

2. What is the difference in God's judgment of your faith vs. works?

_____

_____

_____

3. What words best describe your level of good works over last year?
 Frequent, vibrant   Occasional, intense   Rare, fearful   Zero
What can you do to improve? _____

4. What words best describe your level of giving to God this past year?
Sacrificial Generous 10% Regular Meager Zero
What will you do to improve? _____
Which Scripture motivates you to overcome "affluenza"? _____

5. Have you written and filed a current will?   Yes   No
Will you revise it to include a "rapture clause?"   Yes   No

6. What is the bull's-eye focus of your life? What are you living for?

_____

_____

7. If God were to grade your perseverance, what grade do you think He would give you?   A   B   C+   D–   F

8. What do you want written in your obituary about you? Write it here:

_____

_____

_____

_____

Section Six

Heaven's Rewards Are Waiting

Y ou live in the midst of a postmodern culture at the turn of the third millennium. You are part of the final generation in "the last days" that is seeing eternal prophecies fulfilled with startling accuracy. Christ will likely return to earth in the early part of the twenty-first century.

God wants your anticipation of Christ's return to dramatically impact your life. God's primary purpose for giving prophecy is to inspire you to obey biblical principles in daily living. There is no point in knowing the truth if what you know doesn't change the way you live.

The apostle John wrote in 1 John 2:28, "And now, dear children, continue in him, so that when he appears we may be confident and unashamed before him at his coming."

He explains what he means by this in 1 John 3:2-3:

Dear friends, now we are the children of God, and what we will be has not yet been made known. But we know that when he appears, we shall be like him, for we shall see him as he is. Everyone who has this hope in him purifies himself, just as he is pure.

What does a pure, godly, spotless, blameless, wholly holy life look like? What precisely does Christ ask Christians to do until He comes?

In view of Christ's soon return, five biblical imperatives take on heightened importance. God repeatedly and urgently emphasizes these five primary commands in direct conjunction with passages relating to Christ's return for His church. Those commands are to watch, to witness, to worship, to walk and to work.

The Personal Applicational Reviews that concluded each chapter provided you with specific suggestions for spiritual growth that will, if applied, result in your fuller enjoyment of eternal rewards at the Judgment Seat of Christ.

The purpose of this final section is to paint a permanent picture in your mind regarding the absolute importance of you keeping the commitments that you have now made before the Lord.

◆ Chapter 24 ◆

A Tale of Two Christians

The stories you are about to hear are true. The names have been changed to protect you.

John was a Christian who "prayed the prayer," "walked the aisle," and "followed the Lord in baptism" many years ago. He grew up in a church that emphasized "once saved, always saved." John took a lot of comfort in that promise. In fact, he took so much comfort in it that he drifted into living a rather sloppy spiritual life.

John attended church, but only when he didn't have any more exciting plans for the weekend. He even gave a few donations to the church, but all of it totaled only about two percent of his income. He did agree to help out by being a Greeter at the front doors of the church once or twice a year, but John's commitment to Christ never went much beyond that. After all, he wanted to live this life to the fullest. He had his ticket to heaven secure. He figured he might as well live out this life for all it's worth while he still had the chance.

He worked long hours to earn extra money so he could buy new trucks and fast boats and fly away to a nice exotic vacation spot each year. He drank a little. He cussed and gambled a little. He went to see the latest R-rated movies. He prayed only when he had problems. He rarely read his Bible. Only once did he ever try to witness to somebody about Christ. Since he didn't think of himself as a spiritual leader, he never volunteered for any kind of consistent service within his church.

When John finally died, he went to heaven. God's grace was broad enough to forgive all his sins. God's promise of eternal life proved true.

But as John was entering heaven, he had to stand before the Judgment Seat of Christ. In front of him was a huge pile of stuff, representing John's use of his time, treasure and talent on the earth. At first he was excited. Then an angel lit a match and set his pile of stuff on fire. It roared into a gigantic bonfire that engulfed his pile and could be seen for miles around. When the flames died down, all that was left behind were a couple of little tiny pieces of silver. The angel picked these up, handed them to John, and said, "Here is your reward."

Back on earth, a friend of John's was another Christian, named Mary. Mary was a Christian who trusted Christ just a few years ago. She also grew up in a church that emphasized "once saved, always saved," but she understood what the Bible taught about eternal rewards, so, she determined that she would not drift into a sloppy spiritual life. She made church a high priority, not out of duty, but out of a desire to learn and grow. She made the commitment to tithe a full ten percent of her income to her church. She watched with amazement how God honored His promise to meet all her needs. She read her Bible and prayed about what it said to her each day. She made the commitment to find a weekly area of service for the Lord within her church that fit her spiritual gift. She took advantage of opportunities to share Christ with her friends and neighbors.

After all, she wanted her life to count for eternity, so she invested her life in eternal things while she still had the chance. Sure, she missed out on enjoying a few extravagant pleasures that she could have had, but she, along with Moses in Hebrews 11:25-26:

> chose to be mistreated along with the people of God rather than to enjoy the pleasures of sin for a short time. He regarded disgrace for the sake of Christ as of greater value than the treasures of Egypt, because he was looking ahead to his reward.

When Mary finally died, she went to heaven. There, she found God's promises of eternal rewards to be true. As Mary was entering heaven, she stood before the Judgment Seat of Christ. In front of her was a huge pile of stuff, representing her "works" on the earth. An angel lit a match and set her pile of stuff on fire. It burned for a little while, and then it went out.

Left behind was a large pile of gold, silver and precious stones. Ten angels came along with big wheelbarrows to scoop it all up and to deliver it to Mary's large mansion. Jesus had built this mansion for her out of all the treasures that she had already sent on ahead through her generous giving to the Lord. Jesus Himself walked over to her, and with a big smile on His face, He said, "Well done, my good and faithful servant; enter into the joy of your reward."

When you arrive in heaven, will your experience be like John's, or will it be like Mary's? The choice is entirely yours. You have been given fair warning of what lies ahead. The question is, what difference will this warning make in your life?

You, like John and Mary, are investing your life in something. What is it?

Are you using building materials that will last? When God puts the torch to all the work you have done for Him, will there be anything left besides charred ashes and smoke?

How big will your bonfire be? The pile of your deeds may look impressive now. They may be stacked high. But when the fire dies down, what will be left of that huge stack of "stuff?"

On that day when everything that you have ever done is finally tested by the fire of God, will it endure like precious metals, or will it be reduced to a pile of black ashes?

Before you answer, read the next chapter to learn about the Judgment Seat of Christ.

"*Each one should be careful how he builds ... for the fire will test the quality of each man's work.*"

◆ Chapter 25 ◆

The Judgment Seat of Christ

Did you find yourself identifying with either John or Mary? Those stories in the previous chapter come directly out of what the apostle Paul teaches us in 1 Corinthians 3:10-15:

By the grace God has given me, I laid a foundation as an expert builder, and someone else is building on it. But each one should be careful how he builds. If any man builds on this foundation [of Christ] using gold, silver, costly stones, wood, hay or straw, his work will be shown for what it is, for the Day will bring it to light. It will be revealed by fire, and the fire will test the quality of each man's work. If what he has built survives, he will receive his reward. If it is burned up, he will suffer loss; he himself will be saved, but only as one escaping through the flames.

In the Greek of 1 Corinthians 3:10, Paul calls himself an *architectron,* from which we derive our word "architect." An architect is not only the one who designs a building and draws up the blueprints. He is also the on-the-job foreman who supervises the construction and calls the shots.

Once Paul left Corinth, others came after him to build on his foundation. Apollos came along and put up the stud walls and nailed in the trusses. Then Peter came along and installed the windows and topped off the plumbing. Later on, someone else put on the siding, while another added the insulation, nailed up the sheet rock and painted the walls. At each stage of the project, Paul warns in verse 10, "each one should be careful how he builds."

Gold vs. Straw

In building the church, there are only two kinds of building materials. The first kind is strong and permanent, represented by gold, silver and precious stones. The second kind is weak and temporary, represented by wood, hay and straw. The point of this contrast is that you need to use only the best there is for God's church, not the leftovers. You need to give God the very highest quality, not the cheapest quality, in your work for Him. God's building code for His church states you must carefully avoid all inferior, shoddy workmanship.

Why? Because when Christ returns for you, you will stand before the judgment seat of Christ. At that judgment, He is going to test the quality of your life's works. That will be the basis for His determining how much He will reward you in eternity.

God is a stringent building inspector. The way God will conduct His final inspection of what you've built is that He'll blow-torch it. Anything that was unworthy of Him will go up in smoke. As verse 13 warns, "his work will be shown for what it is . . . It will be revealed with fire, and the fire will test the quality of each man's work."

When it comes to God's evaluation of your contribution to the building up of His kingdom, there will be two kinds of judgments that Christ will hand out. Each one is marked off in the text with the word "If," denoting two possible scenarios.

The first possible scenario is that you will be rewarded for your quality work. 1 Corinthians 3:14 promises, "If what he has built survives, he will receive his reward." If you work to build God's kingdom with right motives in the power of the Spirit, by sharing the gospel, encouraging believers, teaching correct doctrine, loving the unlovely, giving sacrificially and worshiping God from the heart, then God says He is going to reward you for that. In Revelation 22:12, Jesus declares, "Behold, I am coming soon! My reward is with me, and I will give to everyone according to what he has done."

Paul explains God's judgment of believers a bit more in 2 Corinthians 5:9-10:

> So we make it our goal to please [God], whether we are at home in the body or away from it. For we must all appear before the judgment seat of Christ, that each one may receive what is due him for things done while in the body, whether good or bad.

When Is Good 'Good'?

Whether God will judge your service as good or bad will be based on two factors. The first factor is your motives, whether you were trying to glorify the Lord or glorify yourself. The second factor is your power-source, whether you were doing it in the strength of the Holy Spirit or in the strength of your own flesh.

The gold, silver and precious stones are the good "good works" you do in the Spirit which are worthy of Christ. The wood, hay and straw are the bad "good works" you do in the strength of your flesh which are unworthy of Christ. The good "good works" will last, whereas the bad, or worthless "good works" will be burned up in the fire of God's judgment.

For example, if you go door to door handing out tracts to people out of obligation, or out of guilt, or because you want to show that you are better than somebody else, it's wood. But if you do it out of genuine love for the Lord and desire to see people saved, it is gold.

If you sing a solo in church because you want to impress people with your voice, it's hay. But if you sing the same song out of a pure desire to glorify the Lord, it is silver.

If you give generously from your income because you feel pressured by others to do so, it's straw. But if you give cheerfully and joyfully to show your love for Christ and because you desire to reach others with the gospel, it is to

God a precious stone.

Whatever you do to help build God's church, whether it is to preach a sermon, remodel a building, serve in the nursery, teach Sunday School, repair the bus, or whatever, if you are doing it because you love the Lord, you're walking in the Spirit and you truly desire to be obedient to Him, God thinks it is worthy of a reward. But, if you do any of those same things because you want human recognition, or because you are just getting an obligation out of the way so you won't feel guilty about it, God evaluates it as unworthy of Him, as something that deserves to be burned.

In the flesh, it is you doing it, so even when it's good, it's worthless. In the Spirit, it is Christ living in you that is doing it, so even when it is weak, it is strong. When you allow Christ to live His life through you, through the enabling power of the Holy Spirit within you, you cannot (at that moment) be sinning. Therefore, the "secret" to spiritual victory is "not I, but Christ." It is to continually yield to the leading of the Spirit within you as you serve Him.

What is the true motive behind the service you do for God? Is it the love of praise, or sense of responsibility, or personal ambition? Or is it truly because you love Jesus Christ and desire, above all else, to please Him? Is your service for God empowered by His Spirit or by your flesh?

In the end, you will discover that everything which has eternal value in your life has been accomplished not by you, but by Christ working through you.

In that great day when all the universe sees your life for what it really is, when all your secret thoughts and motives are shouted from the housetops, will you be filled with joy because it will be shown that you were a disciple whose true goal was to glorify God? Or, will you slink away and be ashamed that you wasted so many years trying to make a good impression on people, or trying to build up a lot of influence and money and prestige for yourself?

Rewards 101

What kind of rewards will God give? Sometimes the Scriptures describe your rewards as crowns that represent your spiritual achievements. Sometimes they are described as your gaining the privilege to rule over many cities during the millennial kingdom. Sometimes the picture is that you'll live in more intimate fellowship or closer proximity to Jesus in heaven.

One definite part of the reward will be to hear the Lord praise you verbally. He will look at you individually and say, "Well done, good and faithful servant" (Matthew 25:21). For you to be able to experience that full thrill of His approval, that joyful fulfillment of knowing that you have spent your life in a way that counts for eternity, will be a great reward in itself.

The second possible scenario is that you will go to heaven, but will have nothing more beyond that to receive. This is the second "If" in 1 Corinthians 3:15: "If it is burned up, he will suffer loss; he himself will be saved, but only as one escaping through the flames."

Anything you do for the Lord that flows out of your selfish motives and fleshly strength is, as far as God is concerned, nothing but wood, hay and straw. It will be consumed in the flames of judgment because God gives no rewards for shoddy work. Carnal Christians who live for themselves will watch with empty, limp hands as all their life's efforts go up in smoke.

Paul is quick to add that this person will be saved. His eternal security is not threatened. But he will enter heaven as a poor person, as one who just barely escaped by the skin of his teeth, as one who has been pulled out of the burning house just in the nick of time before the rafters caved in.[43]

---

[43]Verse 15 is not talking about some kind of purgatory. This fire is not designed to purify a person of his sins, because Christ already paid all we owe for our sins. Rather, this fire only burns up those works that are not worthy of reward.

The fire is coming. This is God's severe warning. Be alert to recognize it for what it is. The flipside of God's fire of judgment are God's crowns of reward.

The next chapter will explain the basis of these rewards. This is absolutely crucial. It will encourage your soul.

It is the most thrilling message of all!

◆ Chapter 26 ◆

Five Commands, Five Crowns

The Bible teaches that there are five specific areas of obedience that God will reward with crowns in heaven.[44] The "bottom line surprise" of this book is the discovery that these five crowns "just happen" to directly parallel the five W's of watch, witness, worship, walk and work!

That's right! Jesus Christ has purposefully designed heaven's rewards to serve as incentives for you to get ready for His return! When you choose to obey these five commands which He links directly to your anticipation of the rapture, you automatically qualify for five heavenly "sweepstakes," prizes which every obedient disciple is eligible to win.

God's grace is truly amazing. His stipulation for each eternal crown is directly dependent on whether or not you have chosen to obediently get ready for Christ's return by obeying His final commands to the church by watching, witnessing, worshiping, walking and working, until Christ comes.

Jesus Christ has determined that the process of getting ready for Christ's return provides both the key to your eternal rewards in heaven <u>and</u> the key to your spiritual discipleship on earth.

If you choose to focus your Christian life on diligently and obediently watching, witnessing, worshiping, walking

---

[44]David Benoit, "Royal Ambassadors' Endtime Diplomacy," in *Foreshocks of the Antichrist* (Eugene, OR: Harvest House Publishers, 1997), 350-52.

and working in light of Christ's return, your eternal rewards will be amazingly rich. God tells you, His child, that His "secret" to you enjoying the most fabulous "forever" imaginable is that you center your life around your obedience to these five commands.

WATCH to Receive the Crown of Righteousness

God promises that if you watch for the rapture, He will give you the crown of righteousness. 2 Timothy 4:8 declares:

Now there is in store for me the crown of righteousness, which the Lord, the righteous Judge, will award to me on that day—and not only to me, but also to all who have longed for his appearing.

This crown is awarded specifically to those who watch for Christ to return. Christ will reward you with this crown only if you eagerly look forward to seeing His face.

God mentions other rewards for "watching." 1 Corinthians 4:5 says to us:

judge nothing before the appointed time; wait till the Lord comes. He will bring to light what is hidden in darkness and will expose the motives of men's hearts. At that time each will receive his praise from God

If, in light of Christ's soon return, you obey God's command to refrain from judging other Christians, you will hear words of praise from God.

God also promises to reward you for being patient as you wait for God's coming judgment on the evil injustices in the world. James 5:7-9 urges us:

Be patient, then, brothers, until the Lord's coming . . . be patient and stand firm, because the Lord's coming is near. Don't grumble against each other, brothers, or you will be judged. The Judge is standing at the door!

Christ's return could come at any moment. As Jesus assures you in Luke 21:28, "When these things begin to take place, stand up and lift up your heads, because your redemption is drawing near."

Every morning, open your eyes wide and watch for

Him to come. Living each day with that glorious expectation will cause you to live for the smile of your Master, and He will reserve for you a crown of righteousness!

WITNESS to Receive the Crown of Joy

If you as a Christian faithfully witness for Christ before He returns, God will give you the crown of joy. Speaking to the people whom he had led to faith in Christ, Paul says in 1 Thessalonians 2:19, "For what is our hope, our joy, or the crown in which we will glory in the presence of our Lord Jesus when he comes? Is it not you?" Using the same terminology in Philippians 4:1, Paul describes the believers he won to Christ as "my joy and crown."

In John 4:36, Jesus indicates that God rewards those who witness. He says that the "reaper" of souls "draws his wages, even now he harvests the crop for eternal life, so that the sower and the reaper may be glad together." Sowers and reapers will both be paid "wages" by God.

Speaking of the "race of witnessing," 1 Corinthians 9:25 promises an eternal crown. "Everyone who competes in the games goes into strict training. They do it to get a crown that will not last; but we do it to get a crown that will last forever." This is the crown of joy.

Jesus offers lavish rewards to those who boldly witness and win people to faith in Christ. Mark 10:29-30 promises:

no one who has left [anything] for me and the gospel will fail to receive a hundred times as much in this present age . . . and in the age to come, eternal life.

Witness for Christ as you wait for His return and you will receive a crown of joy!

WORSHIP to Receive the Crown of Life

God offers the crown of life to you if you worship Jesus Christ, despite persecution, as you wait for Him to come. James 1:12 teaches:

Blessed is the man who perseveres under trial, because

when he has stood the test, he will receive the crown of life that God has promised to those who love him.

In John 15:13, Jesus defined the greatest love in terms of being willing to die for the one you love. Therefore, the highest form of loving God in worship is your willingness to give up your life for the sake of God's glory. That is why Revelation 2:10 urges, "Be faithful, even to the point of death, and I will give you the crown of life."

Only Christians who have a genuine, sincere, personal life of loving devotion, who worship God to the extent of being willing to die for Him, will qualify to receive this particular crown.

In Matthew 5:10-12, Jesus assures you of great rewards if you willingly sacrifice and suffer because of your identification with Him:

Blessed are those who are persecuted because of righteousness, for theirs is the kingdom of heaven. Blessed are you when people insult you, persecute you and falsely say all kinds of evil against you because of me. Rejoice and be glad, because great is your reward in heaven, for in the same way they persecuted the prophets who were before you.

2 Corinthians 4:17 assures us that "our light and momentary troubles are achieving for us an eternal glory that far outweighs them all." Romans 8:18 adds, "For I consider that our present sufferings are not worth comparing with the glory that will be revealed in us."

In addition to this crown for worshiping Him to the point of suffering and death, God will reward you for worshiping Him by means of faithfully using your God-given abilities to serve others. 1 Peter 4:10 commands, "Each one should use whatever gift he has received to serve others, faithfully administering God's grace in its various forms." This stewardship of your abilities is highly stressed by Jesus in the parables of the minas and talents (in Luke 19:11-26 and Matthew 25:14-24) as being worthy of His reward.

God also will reward you by how consistently you have worshiped Him by using your money as a faithful steward for God's glory. 1 Timothy 6:17-19, 2 Corinthians 9:6-7 and 1 Corinthians 16:2 are but a few passages that stress the importance of being obedient to Christ's specific command to "Put this money to work until I come back" (Luke 19:13).

When you worship your Lord sacrificially, He will give you a crown of life!

WALK to Receive the Crown of Victory

To those who walk with Christ in obedience and holiness, God will give the crown of victory. 2 Timothy 2:5 states, "if anyone competes as an athlete, he does not receive the victor's crown unless he competes according to the rules."

If you want this victor's crown, you must remember that the chief rule of the game of life is to walk worthy of your calling as a child of God (Ephesians 4:1). At the judgment seat of Christ, Jesus will judge and reward you on the basis of how well you have walked with Him in several specific areas:

* God will reward you on the basis of how clear-mindedly you have prayed once you realize that "the end of all things" has begun. 1 Peter 4:7 declares, "The end of all things is near. Therefore be clear minded and self-controlled so that you can pray." Similarly, Matthew 6:10 instructs you to pray "your kingdom come, your will be done on earth as it is in heaven." Your prayers should also include the Bible's final appeal, "Come, Lord Jesus" (Revelation 22:20).

* God will reward you on the basis of how blameless you have been in your love towards Christians and others in view of Christ's return. 1 Thessalonians 3:12-13 states this blessing:

May the Lord make your love increase and overflow
for each other and for everyone else, just as ours does for

you. May he strengthen your hearts so that you will be blameless and holy in the presence of our God and Father when our Lord Jesus comes with all his holy ones.

* God will reward you on the basis of how lovingly you have cared for other believers who are in need. Hebrews 6:10 promises, "God is not unjust; he will not forget your work and the love you have shown him as you have helped his people and continue to help them."

In Matthew 10:41-42, Jesus teaches the same concept:

Anyone who receives a prophet because he is a prophet will receive a prophet's reward, and anyone who receives a righteous man because he is a righteous man will receive a righteous man's reward. And if anyone gives even a cup of cold water to one of these little ones because he is my disciple, I tell you the truth, he will certainly not lose his reward.

* God will reward you on the basis of how diligently you have taught and cared for people whom God has placed under your spiritual authority. Hebrews 13:17 tells you that church leaders "keep watch over you as men who must give an account." James 3:1 reminds you of this: "we who teach will be judged more strictly."

* God will reward you on the basis of how perseveringly you have run that particular race that God has chosen for you to run. Hebrews 12:1 invites, "let us throw off everything that hinders and the sin that so easily entangles, and let us run with perseverance the race marked out for us." Philippians 3:14 presents Paul's example for us to follow: "I press on toward the goal to win the prize . . ."

Each of these criteria for future judgment is related to the crown of victory. Each of them support God's overall plea: walk worthy of your calling as a child of God as you wait for Christ to come!

WORK to Receive the Crown of Glory

In view of Christ's imminent return for His church, God calls leaders to work for God's kingdom with dedicated service. Speaking particularly to those who nurture and protect other Christians as pastors and teachers, God offers the crown of glory. 1 Peter 5:2-4 speaks to Christian leaders who shepherd God's flock as faithful overseers of the church:

Be shepherds of God's flock that is under your care, serving as overseers–not because you must, but because you are willing, as God wants you to be; not greedy for money, but eager to serve; not lording it over those entrusted to you, but being examples to the flock. And when the Chief Shepherd appears, you will receive the crown of glory that will never fade away.

2 Timothy 4:1-2 also urges those who preach God's Word to perform their responsibilities in light of Christ's judgment of their work:

In the presence of God and of Christ Jesus, who will judge the living and the dead, and in view of his appearing and his kingdom, I give you this charge: Preach the Word; be prepared in season and out of season; correct, rebuke and encourage–with great patience and careful instruction.

The crown of glory seems to be restricted to those who have poured their lives into full-time Christian service. If you are a pastor or missionary or other vocational servant of God, you must use your time, treasure and talent to work faithfully for Christ's kingdom until He comes. Why? Because as a reward for your faithful and fruitful labor, you will receive a crown of glory!

Crowns Count

Heaven certainly will be richer for each Christian who is given crowns of reward.

Will God really give out only and exactly five kinds of crowns? No one knows for sure. Yet you cannot dispute the fact that God will give rewards to some Christians but not to others at the judgment seat of Christ. Whether or not you receive any or all of these "crowns" of reward is dependent entirely on the choices that you make from this day forward during the few remaining hours you have left on earth before Christ raptures you to heaven.

The Bible's teaching on eternal rewards goes beyond these five crowns to describe the eternal home that our Savior is now preparing for us in heaven. That is the subject of the next chapter.

You're about to enter the "dessert" portion of this book. You're going to love this!

• Chapter 27 •

Glimpse Into Eternity

A little boy was sitting on his grandpa's knee in front of a mirror and asked, "Grandpa, who made me?" The man replied, "God did." "Who made Daddy?" "God did." "Who made you?" "Well, God made me, too."

The boy looked in the mirror, then back at his wrinkled grandpa, and said with great confidence, "It sure seems as though God has been doing a better job in recent years."

When God does something new, He always does it better. When God brings us into our heavenly home, it will be even more beautiful than our earthly home. He Himself will thoroughly wipe away all the hurt and pain of past suffering and grief. We'll never have any reason to ever cry again. Everything old will be made new, and all your wrinkles and zits and crow's feet will be gone!

The Bible calls the New Jerusalem, our heaven, both a bride and a city. A bride speaks of intimacy and a city speaks of community. The picture is that all the redeemed people of God, each one living in a glorious body empowered with limitless energy, will live in close intimacy with God and in community with each other forever. Revelation 21:3-4 is especially comforting:

> And I heard a loud voice from the throne saying, 'Now the dwelling of God is with men, and he will live with them. They will be his people, and God himself will be with them and be their God. He will wipe every tear from their eyes. There will be no more death or mourning or crying or pain, for the old order of things has passed away.'

Jeweler's Fantasy

The New Jerusalem is a jeweler's fantasy, an absolutely stunning sight. John saw a cube-shaped city with three foundations on each side and a gate above each foundation. The overall appearance of this city is like a brilliant wedding ring, for the jasper stone, the most expensive gem imaginable, is a diamond that shines like a clear crystal. Words are inadequate to describe it.

John felt overawed and stunned by the beauty and majesty of this heavenly city. Excitement filled his heart as he realized that this will be the eternal home of all believers.[45]

How Big Is Heaven?

Try to imagine the immense size of this city. According to Revelation 21:16, it is a square city that is about 1,400 miles long and 1,400 miles wide. If you set it down on top of a map of the United States, it would cover two-thirds of the United States, stretching from Seattle over to Chicago and down to the southern tip of Texas. By another comparison, since the moon is only 2160 miles in diameter, this heavenly city will be two-thirds the size of the moon.

Allowing fifteen feet per story, the New Jerusalem will be over 500,000 stories high. Each of these 500,000 stories will contain two million square miles; and all the stories combined will total about a trillion square miles. In such a city there would be ample room for a total population of over 100 trillion people.

Is that big enough? I estimate that less than 15 billion people have ever lived since Adam (six billion are alive as of 2000), and only a small portion of these will be saved.

---

[45]Some Bible teachers contend that this city, the "new Jerusalem," will be suspended over the earth during the millennium, hovering over the old earth like a satellite. It is simpler to assume this city will not appear until after the millennial kingdom has been completed, when the eternal state begins with a new heaven and new earth.

So, there will be so much room it might seem like we're a bunch of BBs rattling around inside a basketball.

Rest assured, there will be no claustrophobia in heaven. The new earth will have plenty of room for lush snow-capped mountains and large fresh water lakes, crystal clear rivers and evergreen fruit trees, meadows of flowers and towering waterfalls. No one will be the least bit disappointed by what they find there. There will be unlimited places to go and gadzillions of things to do.

Streets of Gold

Twice, we are told that the streets of heaven are made of transparent one hundred percent pure gold (Revelation 21:18,21). You can see right through them, like glass. Such gold in heaven will be as commonplace as asphalt and cement are to us.

Throughout history and around the world, gold has always been the universal standard for establishing monetary value. That's because it is a scarce commodity. If you took all the gold in the world and put it all together in one place, it could all be contained within a cube that is only eighteen yards wide on each side. That is not just all the gold in America, but in the world.

All the gold in every watch, ring and necklace, in every vault, in every brick and coin in every museum, in every false tooth, and in every gold-plated object, all put together in pure form would pile up only one-tenth the size of the Washington Monument. That is the sum total of six thousand years of digging, scratching, panning, stripping and dredging the earth. That is all there is. Yet in the New Jerusalem, the heavenly city, God will have so much gold, He will pave the streets with it just to get rid of it! How foolish is the person who makes gold his god.

Have you heard the story of the man who finally figured out a way to "take it with him" when he died? When he arrived in heaven, his bags were filled with lots of twenty-four carat gold, just as he had planned. But as he was being welcomed into heaven, an angel asked him, "Of all the things you could have brought with you, why did you bring pavement?"

Pearls of Great Price

Revelation 21:21 tells us that the gates of heaven are made of huge single pearls. You have heard many jokes about St. Peter and the pearly gates, as if there is only a single large pair of gates. Here we find that there actually are twelve pearly gates, and St. Peter is nowhere to be seen guarding any of them. [So much for the jokes!]

Since each gate is made from one gigantic pearl, it makes you wonder if God might have some huge oysters living somewhere in His universe making these huge pearls. After all, the pearl is unique among all other precious gems in that it is made within a living organism. A pearl is formed when a tiny grain of sand gets inside an oyster's shell, which to the oyster feels like crackers in bed. So to relieve its pain, it covers this irritant with a soft lustrous solution that hardens into a beautiful, glowing pearl. In a poetic way, a pearl speaks of beauty out of pain, because its beauty arises out of the pain of an irritated oyster.

That process spiritually describes how God made us beautiful through the pain of Jesus. The beauty of the pearl of great price, the church, came out of the pain that Christ suffered for us as He went through the terrible anguish of the cross for us. He suffered in order to cover over our sin, which irritated Him, with His perfect blood. The fact that the gates of heaven are made of pearls will remind us throughout eternity that we were once a little grain of sharp, dirty sand that was causing pain in the side of Christ. But Christ took that painful thing and covered it with His perfect, soft righteousness. Our beauty is not in us, the grain of sand, but in His righteousness that Christ puts around us by His grace.

Diamonds, gold, pearls. Can you begin to imagine how

heaven is going to look?

Gleaming transparent gold, with twelve foundations sparkling with light in cascading colors, pouring forth from gigantic jewels embedded in every side like a kaleidoscope of light and glory, an intensely bright rainbow, giving a fantastic and brilliant coloring to the new universe. This multi-colored display will be absolutely dazzling, fabulous and breathtaking.

Unimaginable Thrills

Heaven will not be a bland, sterile, dull and colorless place. It will be thrilling to see it. It will cause you to gasp in awe. It will be far more beautiful than anything that man has ever been able to design. It will reflect the glory of God in a spectrum of brilliant colorful light forever.

It will be so utterly startling that it would immediately bring tears to your eyes and put a lump in your throat, if only you could see it now.

Heaven will be an absolutely amazing place to be. The Hebrew and Greek words for "heaven" both mean "highest heights," for it is the apex of the universe. Heaven is a real place. It's not a state of mind. It's not a figment of man's imagination. It's not a philosophical concept. It's not a religious abstraction. It's not a sentimental dream. It's not the medieval fancy of an ancient scientist. It's not the worn-out superstition of theologians.

It is a real location that is far more real than what you see around you right now.[46]

What will you do there? You won't sit around listening to the hallelujah chorus every hour of every day for fifty centuries. With a perfect mind and a perfect body, you will constantly have enough energy to develop your human capacities to their fullest potential. You will be able to

---

[46]Many of these descriptions come from Steven J. Lawson, *Heaven Help Us!* (Colorado Springs, CO: NavPress, 1995), 16.

create a poem or paint a gorgeous landscape or sing a solo with perfect pitch. Geographers will be able to survey a continent at a glance. Astronomers will be able to explore a solar system in a day. Historians will be able to review the detailed events of a century in one sitting. Physicists, craftsmen, mathematicians, will be able to forever explore and perfect their work without getting tired and without making mistakes. What about doctors and nurses and respiratory therapists? They'll all be out of their jobs! So will preachers! But there still will be a vast world of reality for them to study and explore.

Ultimate Fulfillment

Heaven will be a place of no more unanswered questions, no more disturbing doubts and no more unsolvable mysteries. The sub-atomic structure of the atom will be child's play compared to what we'll learn there. There will be no more ignorance, no more anguished "whys?", for there you will know fully, even as you are fully known by God. Heaven will be a place of complete and perfect rest, no worries, no hurries, no delays, no lack of time to finish the job right, no time clocks to punch, no alarm clocks to wake you up.

Heaven is a place where those who were lifelong invalids on earth will have bodies that pulsate with vibrant health, with no more headaches, no more backaches, no more fatigue. Those bowed down with the infirmities of old age now will become immortal athletes, forever young again. There will be a lot to see, and it will take you ages to see it all as you walk along on streets of gold. There will be a lot to eat for enjoyment, and you'll never gain weight. There will be no more sorrow, no more crying, no more death. And your greatest joy will be in constantly seeing those individuals in heaven whom you personally helped lead to faith in Christ so they could be saved.

Will you be able to recognize your loved ones? Of course you will! Didn't Paul tell us in 1 Thessalonians 4 that the assurance of our reunion with loved ones in the rapture would bring us comfort? Did not Peter, James and John immediately know who Moses and Elijah were on the Mount of Transfiguration, even though they had never seen them before?

In the same way, your loved ones will recognize you instantly, because in heaven, the uniqueness of your individuality is preserved. When Christ resurrects your body, He's going to restore your basic appearance–only with the flaws removed–and you are going to be radiantly beautiful.

Heaven will be a place where free, beautiful homes will be given away in a perfect city. That home comes equipped with pure water, no electric bills, free perpetual lighting, perfect health guaranteed, complete immunity from accidents, beautiful music and no taxes.

Heaven will not be a stuffy, rigid, formal place, because heaven will be your HOME – your home sweet home – your beautiful, everlasting home. It will be a satisfying, gratifying eternal home where you will reign as kings and queens forever with your God. As 1 John 3:2 states, when we finally see Christ, we shall be like Him, for we shall see Him as He is, face to face. Psalm 16:11 affirms, in God's presence is fullness of joy, and at His right hand are pleasures evermore.

Sometimes I get homesick for heaven–don't you? Once there, we'll no longer have to fret about poverty or illness. We'll no longer need to worry about abortion rights, the threat of nuclear terrorism, the balance of trade or the national debt. There will be no more farewells with swollen eyes and tear-stained cheeks. Our hopes will be fulfilled, our happiness will be bliss, our rest will be peaceful and our knowledge will be full. Our life there will never be monotonous or dull.

We cannot even imagine all the wonderful things God has prepared for those who love Him.

Maximum Impact

Do you want your life to significantly count for the Lord? Do you long to make a lasting maximum impact for His kingdom? Do you desire to be available for the Lord Jesus Christ to use your life for His eternal glory any way He sees fit? Are you sold-out to be a totally devoted disciple of Jesus? Do you desire to experience the glories of eternity to the max?

Really?

Then commit yourself to lead a "Five W" kind of life. Be a person who maintains your focus on watching, witnessing, worshipping, walking and working until Christ comes.

Get ready to seriously apply what you are about to read in the final chapter. Get ready to accept the challenge to devise a personal plan for growth.

♦ Chapter 28 ♦

Your Personal Plan for Growth

The vast majority of Christians go from cradle to grave without ever designing a plan for their own personal growth towards Christlikeness. They spend their entire lives accumulating stuff that will burn but make no plans to acquire an inheritance that will last forever. The average man does not know what to do with this life, yet wants another one that will last forever.[47]

My appeal to you is, don't be average. Don't move with the mob. Choose to take the wiser course, even though that puts you in the minority. Decide what you want to do both with this life and the next one, and then design a definite plan to achieve it.

Don't be lazy and apathetic about your future on earth and in heaven. Take Christ's words seriously. Be willing to pay the price to obey Him and to live by faith.

It's too late to look for someone else to blame for why your life so far hasn't turned out the way you wanted it to be. You cannot afford to take the time to hunt for excuses for your own bad attitudes or poor performance. Take responsibility for your own life and choose to do what you know is right in order to please your Lord.

Quit saying things like, "That's good enough to get by," or "Don't worry, no one will ever notice," or "Nobody's perfect," or "Everybody's doing it," or "What will I get out of it?" Don't be slothful and selfish when it comes to

---

[47] I owe these ideas to the exhortations I've received from Dr. John C. Maxwell of Injoy Ministries.

charting out the course of your life from this point on. Don't let "maintaining the status quo" be good enough for you. Don't let mediocrity be your standard. Aim high. Choose to walk in Jesus' footsteps, cooperating with God's plan to conform your character to His, exercising deliberate effort and using a specific plan.

When Christ returns for you in the rapture, He is not going to say to you, "Hey, I was just kidding about hell, and about the necessity of making your life count for eternity. I didn't really expect you to do anything with the Great Commission. All along, I knew it would be too hard for you to keep all those commands and high standards. I just wrote them for those "hot dogs" who wanted to be missionaries, not for you. So, all is forgiven. Let's party!"

No, Jesus won't say that. Instead, He will ask you to stand before His Judgment Seat. He will ask you about how well you obeyed His commands. He really will set the level of your permanent status of wealth and authority in heaven based solely on your faithful obedience (or lack of it) during your short pilgrimage here on earth.

The purpose of obeying God is not to selfishly enjoy eternal rewards. The purpose is to please your Lord by faith in order to express your intense love and gratitude for all He has done for you. Yet, God knows that you are motivated by the prospect of rewards. He created you that way.

Do not allow a "nay-sayer" Christian to "pooh-pooh" your desire for a luxurious eternity. God is the one who placed a tugging desire for "eternity in your heart" (Ecclesiastes 3:11).

If someone claims that a "Five W" life is "selfish," challenge him to live it and then assess how "selfish" it feels to him!

"Five W" Strategy

The "Five W" Christian is one who keeps a balanced emphasis on watching, witnessing, worshipping, walking and working until Christ comes. This is a Christian who leads a life of fervent faith, radiant hope and sacrificial love.

God designed this to be the "normal" Christian life. However, it is rarely lived.

Why? Because most people think that it is "too hard."

The truth is, a "Five W" life is hard. But it also is well worth the effort. Nothing you will ever experience in time or eternity will feel as good as to one day hear Jesus Christ say to you, "Well done, good and faithful servant! You have been faithful with a few things; I will put you in charge of many things. Come and share your master's happiness!" (Matthew 25:21)

The greatest of all thrills will be to one day find yourself basking in the approval of your Lord saying to you, "You lived your life right; you obeyed my Word from the heart; you did very well in using what I gave to you just the way I had asked you to do. You watched for My return, your witnessed for Me, you worshiped Me, you walked with me and you worked for me. Good job! You have proven your love for Me by obeying My commands."

Do you long to hear those words from your Creator and Lord? Then do not just close this book and put it on the shelf. Take the time and effort to allow its truths to radically revolutionize your life. Honestly assess where you are now, set your sights on where you want to be, and develop a workable strategy that will enable your life to move from where you are to where you want to be.

Probe your own soul with these penetrating questions: Do the spokes of your life radiate from the strong hub of Jesus? Do you have a solid and growing relationship with Him? Are you living in full obedience to His revealed will?

If your answer to any of these questions is "no," take the time you need to realign your heart with His.

Contrary to the lies of our culture, the "good life" does not consist in the accumulation of material possessions, the acquisition of power, or the enjoyment of sensual pleasure and entertainment. The "good life" really consists in knowing and loving and obeying Jesus Christ. The key to a fulfilling life is to have a personal relationship with Him as your Lord.

Without Him at the center of your life, everything else in your life will be a "trivial pursuit" that will end only in emptiness, frustration and death.

Reckoning With Reality

Face it. We who live in the United States are terribly spoiled. This is a cream-puff country where, for the most part, our daily lives are marked by ease, comfort, convenience and freedom. Compared with other nations scarred by war, poverty, hunger and religious persecution, we enjoy soft and cushy lives. That explains why we react so strongly to our small problems. We are hypersensitive to suffering. When a relatively tiny trial rolls our way and messes up our plans for a few days, we cry and whimper, "Why me, Lord? Why must I suffer so much?"

Such a reaction reveals that spoiled Americans tend to have a warped view of God. We expect God to be like Santa Claus, the Tooth Fairy, and a Rich Uncle all rolled up into one, always handing out money and candy. We want a genie to grant our wishes and gratify our immediate selfish desires for health and wealth, helping us in our scramble to the top of the pile.

The only problem is, this does not describe the God of the Bible. The real God does not exist for the purpose of making our lives easier and more comfortable by catering to our whims.

Naturally, we all prefer to have only pleasant experiences and avoid all unpleasant ones. We'd rather cozy up to what's familiar and shun anything that nudges us in the direction of change or growth. We all gravitate toward pleasure and push away from pain. It's always easier to watch TV or surf the web than it is to study our

Bibles and pray. We feel much more comfortable talking sports with our neighbors than we do sharing the gospel with them.

Yet, in order for you to become a Christian who is truly like Christ, you need to willingly embrace His challenge to live a "Five W" life.

Can you recite those five commands from memory?

Christ calls you to W_____, W_____, W_____, W_____, and W_____ until He comes.

The future king of this world desires and deserves to be the undisputed King of your life from this day forward. He wants you to live each day in light of His imminent return.

Will you permit Him to rule from the throne of your heart? Will you step aside from the control center of your life and let Him be your absolute Lord?

Specifically, what will that look like in your life? Now that you've read this book, what will you do differently to:

WATCH more attentively?

WITNESS more effectively?

WORSHIP more fervently?

WALK more obediently?

WORK more sacrificially?

Write down your personal plan. Set your goals. Then ask a friend to hold you accountable to follow it through.

You could be in the presence of Jesus Christ before this day is through. It's true. Whether the end comes by death or by rapture, today could be your last. Live your life accordingly! Decide now that you will begin each morning with the persistent, nagging thought, "perhaps He will come today!"

When He comes, I'm sure I'll be able to recognize you. You'll be the one screaming victory praises at the top of your resurrected lungs and grinning from ear to ear.

◆ PERSONAL APPLICATIONAL REVIEW ◆

1. Which person best describes you?   John   Mary   In between

2. When you do "good works" for God, are they usually done . . .
for God's glory?   with mixed motives?   for your own glory?

3. If Christ were to take you home today, which crowns would you
receive? Righteousness Joy Life Victory Glory
If you make changes in your life starting now, and the rapture is
delayed for another ten years, check which crowns you hope to qualify
for by then: Righteousness   Joy   Life   Victory   Glory

4. Number these five commands in order of 1 (strongest) to 5 (weakest)
in your own present spiritual life:
Watch   Witness   Worship   Walk   Work

_____   _____   _____   _____   _____

Circle two areas that you plan to improve the most this coming year.

5. This chapter concluded with a challenge to develop a plan to enable
you to grow in Christlike maturity in this life and be assured of greater
rewards in the next life. What's your plan? Brainstorm your ideas here:
My plan to grow in Christlike maturity on earth:

_____

_____

My plan to receive greater rewards in heaven:

_____

_____

6. Take five minutes now to pray for God to lead you into obedience in
your new desires for a life discipleship that fully pleases your coming
Lord. Write your prayer here:

_____

_____

_____

_____

Appendix A

The Best News in the World

Are you absolutely certain that you will go to heaven when you die? Are you totally confident that you have securely received God's gift of eternal life? Do you have the assurance that you are saved, that when Jesus Christ comes back, He's coming for you?

If not, read on.

If you were to die tonight and you found yourself standing before God, and God were to ask you, "Why should I let you into My heaven?," what would you say?

If your answer is that you have tried to be a good person, I'm sorry, but that's not good enough. Not one of us is good enough to make it to heaven, because we have all sinned and fallen short of God's perfect standards. You cannot possibly make it to heaven on your own merits, because what you really deserve is hell. But because God loves you with an everlasting love, He provided a way for sinners like you to go to heaven.

John 3:16 says, "For God so loved the world that he gave his one and only Son, that whoever believes in him shall not perish but have eternal life." Jesus says in John 14:6, "I am the way and the truth and the life. No one comes to the Father except through me."

Eternal life is gained only one way–by having a relationship with God through personally knowing Jesus Christ. But, you may ask, "why do I need a personal relationship with Christ?"

The Bible teaches that you, like all people, have sinned and fall short of the glory of God (Romans 3:23). The wages of your sin is death, which is eternal separation from

God (Romans 6:23). Sin is a dreaded, terminal disease. Left
untreated, it will kill you and send you to hell. But God
loves you so much that He offers you a remedy that can
cleanse your guilt by removing the penalty of your sin. The
only way that you can receive God's cure is to
acknowledge the fact that you cannot earn it and that you
do not deserve it. That remedy is that Christ volunteered to
die in your place. He paid the full debt of your sin as your
substitute, suffering in His own body all the punishment
that you deserved for all your wrongdoing (Romans 5:8).

In Christ, salvation is a done deal. It is finished.
Nothing can be added to it and nothing can improve on it.
If you put your trust in His death and resurrection as the
only basis of your salvation, God will give you the free gift
of eternal life in heaven (Romans 10:9-13). Once you
receive Christ into your life by faith, He becomes your
Savior, your Lord and your Friend.

It's difficult for finite, time-bound creatures like us to
comprehend what eternity will be like. Describing it is like
trying to explain space travel to a worm. But the fact is,
God created you as an immortal creature. That doesn't
mean you will merely endure an endless ongoing existence,
hanging out in space, floating in some limbo forever and
ever. Rather, it means that after your body stops
functioning, your immortal spirit will live on forever in one
of two places—either in the eternal bliss of heaven or in the
eternal agony of hell. The choice is yours.

~ ~ ~

Maybe you're shaking your head, thinking, "I've tried
religion and it didn't work for me. I've read the Bible, I've
tried to pray, I've sat in a pew—but something didn't click."

Is it possible that you went to church but didn't really
ever go to Christ? Could it be that you tried religion, but
haven't really tried a relationship with the living Lord?
Jesus invites you to come to Him, not to the confessional
booth, not to a church building with a steeple on top, not to
a pastor or Bible teacher, but to Him. Not religion, but

relationship. Not Churchianity, but Christ.

Before you can have a relationship with Him, two things are required. One, you must admit that you do not yet have a real relationship with Him, and that you do need one. Two, you must decide to trust His grace alone for your salvation.

~ ~ ~

An event happened many years ago which illustrates the selfless and sacrificial character of God's grace. Mr. Peters worked for the railroad as a drawbridge operator. The railroad crossed a river that was used by large commercial ships. His job was to raise the drawbridge to let the ships pass through, and then to lower it again so that the train could use it to cross the river.

Mr. Peters also had a four year-old son –his only son– whom he loved as much as his own life. Often, he brought his son with him to work.

One day, just after Mr. Peters had raised the drawbridge to let a ship pass through, he received a call on the radio that the three hundred-passenger train would be there in three minutes. Mr. Peters didn't have any time to spare, so be began immediately to lower the bridge. When the bridge was two-thirds the way down, he thought of his son. Feeling panicky inside, he began frantically looking for him.

Finally, he spotted him. The thing he feared most was true. His son had been over by the bridge when it was up, and was now happily playing with some baby birds that he had found underneath the edge of it. If the bridge continued to come down, it would certainly crush him to death, for there would be no way of escape. But if the bridge were not fully down, the three hundred passengers on the train would surely die as the train would crash, derail and fall into the river far below.

It was too late to stop the train. Mr. Peters yelled as loudly as he could to his son to warn him of the danger he was in. Apparently, he was not able to hear because of the noise of the approaching train, because he didn't respond.

Mr. Peters had a split-second choice to make—either the life of his only son, or the lives of the three hundred people on the train. It was a choice between breaking his own heart or breaking the hearts of the thousands of people related to those on the train. Mr. Peters chose to selflessly and sacrificially break his own heart—by continuing to lower the bridge.

God took no pleasure in the death of His Son. It broke His heart. Yet God loved the world. He loved each individual among the multiplied billions of people who ever lived upon this planet, people who were heading for eternal disaster. That is why God the Father allowed His Son to be crushed to death by the accumulated weight of the sins of mankind. God the Father gave His Son to suffer and die in order to take away the penalty of sin from the world.

Jesus Christ has already received the full punishment for your sins, in your place, as your substitute. God has already punished Jesus for your sins, and God will never punish the same sins twice. Once you believe in your heart that Christ has already suffered the agonies of hell for your sins, you receive complete forgiveness from God. God takes your sins and casts them into the depths of the sea, then puts up a sign that says, "No Fishing!"

~ ~ ~

God has already written your pardon from the sentence of judgment for your sins, but in order for your pardon to take effect, you must personally accept your pardon from God.

In 1829, a man named George Wilson, of Philadelphia, committed an act of robbery from the U.S. Mail, killing another person. He was arrested, brought to trial and found guilty. The judge sentenced him to be hanged. Some friends intervened on his behalf, and were finally able to obtain a pardon for him from President Andrew Jackson.

But when he was informed of his pardon, George Wilson refused to accept it.

The sheriff didn't know what to do, for he reasoned, how could he hang a pardoned man? The question was sent to President Jackson, and the perplexed President turned to the U.S. Supreme Count to decide the case. Chief Justice Marshall gave this ruling:

A pardon is a piece of paper, the value of which depends upon its acceptance by the person implicated. It is hardly to be supposed that a person under the sentence of death would refuse to accept a pardon, but if it is refused, it is no pardon. George Wilson must be hanged.

Soon after this ruling, George Wilson was executed, with his pardon lying on the sheriff's desk.

Will you accept your pardon by trusting Christ as your Savior right now? Jesus Christ promises in John 5:24, "I tell you the truth, whoever hears my word and believes him who sent me has eternal life and will not be condemned; he has crossed over from death to life." 1 John 5:13 says:

I write these things to you who believe in the name of the Son of God so that you may know that you have eternal life.

~ ~ ~

In order to receive God's grace and know for certain that you have a salvation that is free, forgiving and forever, express your decision by saying this prayer to God:

"Dear God, I need your grace. I know I am a sinner. I repent of my sin. I need to be forgiven. I need to know that I will forever live with you. I believe that you love me.

I believe that you loved me so much that you sent Your Son, Jesus Christ, to this world. I believe He died in my place, suffering the penalty for my sin, so that I could be forgiven by You. I believe that You raised Him up from the dead and that He is alive and able to save me today.

By faith, I receive Him as my Savior. I believe that He is the only true Lord. By your grace, save me from hell and make me a child of Yours.

I want to be a real Christian, beginning today. Thank you for forgiving me for all my sins. Thank you for freely giving to me the gift of eternal life. Help me to become the kind of person that You want me to be. AMEN."

~ ~ ~

Did you pray that prayer to God with a sincere heart? If so, I encourage you to persevere on your journey through your Christian life. Rest in the assurance of your salvation. Find a growing, evangelical church to attend and ask to be baptized. Communicate with God each day through Bible reading and prayer. Commit yourself to be discipled by a more mature believer who will keep you accountable for continued spiritual growth. Tell your family and friends about the gospel, witnessing to them about what Christ has done for you. Trust and obey Jesus Christ in everything you do. Never stop loving and serving the One who died for you.

And when you get to heaven, look me up! There will be a place at my table for you.

Appendix B

You Can Understand Prophecy

A group of young men met together in a school gym one night a week to play basketball. Each week, the school janitor would sit and read his Bible while he waited patiently for them to finish their game. One evening, one of the men stopped to ask him what he was studying. The old man answered, "the book of Revelation."

Surprised, the young man asked the elderly janitor if he understood such a complicated book.

"Oh yes!" the man replied, "I understand it. It says that Jesus is gonna win!"

That is what prophecy is all about. The prophecies in the Bible tells us about a coming world leader who will at last bring peace and order to our troubled globe to replace all the chaos and confusion that now plague this planet. The name of that leader is not antichrist; it is Jesus Christ. Antichrist will rule the earth for seven years, but Jesus Christ will defeat him and then rule the earth for a thousand years. It's true. "Jesus is gonna win!" You can bet your life on it.

Professional prognosticators and futurologists correctly "predict" the future about thirty to forty percent of the time. In stark contrast, God's "batting average" is a perfect 1.000. Not one of His prophecies has ever been a "dud." You can have total, unwavering confidence that every other prophecy that is still yet to come will likewise be a sure-fire "home run."

How can you know that? 2 Peter 1:20-21 teaches:

Above all, you must understand that no prophecy of Scripture came about by the prophet's own interpretation.

For prophecy never had its origin in the will of man, but men spoke from God as they were carried along by the Holy Spirit.

All Bible prophecies originate directly from God. They unfold in history in a literal, precise and accurate way, with perfect precision, right on schedule. Not one of them can ever fail.[48]

Here are some important definitions for prophetic terms:

RAPTURE. The word "rapture," while not found in our English Bibles, comes from the Latin word *rapio,* which means "to snatch; to seize; to catch away." Jesus Christ will suddenly and unexpectedly enter our upper atmosphere, hovering over the earth in the clouds, and call for His Bride, the church, to meet Him in the air. All true Christians living on earth will be instantaneously "airlifted" to heaven by Christ. 1 Corinthians 15:52 says this will happen "in a flash, in the twinkling of an eye . . . the dead will be raised imperishable, and we will be changed." Christians who are alive at the time of the rapture will be transported to heaven without ever experiencing death. 1 Thessalonians 4:17 says they "will be caught up together with them in the clouds to meet the Lord in the air." I expect Christ to remove His church from the earth shortly before the cataclysmic forces of the seven-year tribulation begin (Revelation 3:10).

ANTICHRIST. The Bible clearly predicts in Revelation 13 that an incredibly popular and powerful world leader will arise to lead the world after the rapture. This "beast" will be acclaimed as a savior or messiah who will rescue the nations from chaos. He will provide such

---

[48]According to the laws of probability, it would require two hundred billion earths, each populated with five billion people, to come up with one person who could make one hundred accurate prophecies without any errors in sequence. Yet when it comes to the Old Testament prophecies concerning the first coming of Christ, the Bible contains not one hundred but three hundred prophecies that all came true in a literal way.

wise and firm direction that earth's population will enthusiastically embrace him as their one world ruler.

TRIBULATION. Sometime after the rapture, the antichrist will make a seven-year peace treaty with Israel (Daniel 9:27). The first half of these seven years will be peaceful and prosperous. The revived Roman Empire will come to power in Europe and create a powerful alliance between the world government and world religion. 144,000 Jewish believers will be busy preaching the gospel throughout the world. Unsaved people will assume that "peace and safety" is here to stay.

Three and a half years later, in the middle of these seven years, things will change drastically. The antichrist will demand that the entire world worship him. To force it, he will impose an economic "mark of the beast" universally that will establish people's allegiance to the beast.

In response to this idolatrous evil, God will unleash His holy wrath through three waves of judgment, the seals, the trumpets and the bowls during the final three and a half years (called "the day of the Lord"). The antichrist will attack and destroy the apostate world church and will exterminate two-thirds of all the Jews. In response, God will bombard the earth-dwellers with intense waves of punishment for their rebellion against Him, decisively defeating all foes.

ARMAGEDDON. At the end of the tribulation, the nations of the world will gather for World War III at a place known as Armageddon. Christ will descend slowly from heaven to earth with His saints. All of mankind's nuclear arsenal and cruise missiles will be aimed at each other, ready for the final battle, but once they see Christ coming through the atmosphere, they will turn their missiles to the sky and attack Him and His white-robed army, just like they would attack an incoming asteroid. All their weapons will be utterly useless against Christ's sovereign power.

MILLENNIUM. God will install His chosen King,

Jesus Christ, on the throne of David in the city of Jerusalem, to rule as the omnipotent dictator over the earth for one thousand years of peace (Revelation 20:1-6). All of God's promises to Israel will at last have their full and literal fulfillment. Christ will literally reign on earth as its supreme political and spiritual leader. Disease will be totally eliminated. The curse of sin will be removed from the physical earth. Human life-spans will be extended for hundreds of years (Isaiah 65:20). Jerusalem will be the capital of a perfect universal government in which war will not exist (Isaiah 2:3,4). This is the utopian "Kingdom" we pray will come so that God's will may be done on earth as it is in heaven.

JUDGMENT. After the one thousand years is completed, there will be one final rebellion led by Satan. This will be followed by Gods' Great White Throne Judgment when all the unsaved are cast into the lake of fire, which is hell. Then God will create a new earth and bring the city of heaven down to rest upon the new earth forever. Believers will enjoy eternity in the presence of the Lord.

When Will the Rapture Occur?

One of the most hotly contested theological debates of our generation is, when will the rapture of the church take place? Here are ten reasons why I expect a pretribulational rapture.

One: IMMINENT RAPTURE. The Bible indicates that there will be no specific signs or warnings to enable a person to accurately predict a date for the rapture (John 14:1-3; 21:21-23; 1 Thessalonians 4:18; Philippians 3:20-21; Titus 2:13). It can occur at any time, without warning.

Two: A BLESSED HOPE. Our expectancy of reunion with Christ (Acts 1:11; 1 Corinthians 15:51-52; Colossians 3:4; 1 Thessalonians 1:10; 1 Timothy 6:14; James 5:7-9; 1 Peter 3:3-4) encourages us to look forward to seeing Christ at any moment, rather than seeing the antichrist.

Three: ELDERS IN HEAVEN. In Revelation 4:4; 5:8;

and 19:7-11 24, crowned human elders sitting on thrones represent the rewarded church in heaven before the tribulation begins.

Four: CONTRASTS WITH SECOND COMING. Many differences can be discerned between the rapture and the second coming of Christ. Christ comes for His Bride, to bring her to heaven to marry her in His Father's house. In contrast, at His second coming, Christ comes with His Bride, to bring her back to earth and to judge the unsaved world and rule over His kingdom from Jerusalem. After the rapture, only unbelievers will be left on earth. After the second coming of Christ to the earth, only believers will be left on earth. Paul's vivid description of the departure of the church from earth in 1 Thessalonians 4:16-17 indicates not that we go up and then immediately back down to earth, as though we are on an elevator, but stay with the Lord, in the air, forever.

Five: NO CHURCH IN REVELATION 6-18. Throughout Revelation 6-18, which describes the tribulation, there are no references to the church or to the Bride of Christ at all. This is a loud silence, a very conspicuous absence. Revelation 13:9, spoken during the reign of antichrist, warns us, "He who has an ear, let him hear." A very similar exhortation is found seven times in Revelation 2 and 3, only there it says, "He who has an ear, let him hear what the Spirit says to the churches." The omission of the phrase "to the churches" in 13:9 is significant because it implies that the church, the body of Christ has already been raptured away.

Six: BABIES IN THE MILLENNIUM. A logical reason for believing in a pre-tribulation rapture is the issue of "Who is going to be left behind to populate the millennial kingdom?" If all believers are raptured just before God's final judgments when all His enemies are destroyed, there would be no one left on earth to have babies to populate the millennial kingdom. All of the saved will be in their resurrected glorified bodies, and they can't have babies anymore, because glorified bodies no longer reproduce (Mark 12:25). All of the unsaved who are judged to be unworthy to remain alive on earth will be punished with death (as described in Matthew 25). However, during the thousand-year reign of Christ on earth, Isaiah 65:20 states that many babies will be born. That is only possible if there are saved people still on earth in their natural bodies when Christ returns to the earth. Those who have babies during the millennium are saved after the rapture and remain alive after Christ's return to earth.

Seven: FOCUS ON ISRAEL. The tribulation is called "the time of Jacob's trouble" (Jeremiah 30:7; Daniel 9:24). God resumes focusing His attention on Israel instead of the Church.

Eight: JEWISH WEDDING STAGES. The seven stages of a Jewish wedding directly parallel a pretribulational rapture. Once a betrothal covenant was made (=Lord's Supper), the bridegroom returned to his father's house to prepare living accommodations for his bride by building her a home. This is what Jesus said He would do for us in John 14:2-3. Christ did not say He would come back and join His Bride so that they could be together where she is (on earth), but that He would bring her to where He was, which is at His Father's house in heaven.

Nine: KEPT FROM THE HOUR OF TRIAL. Before a nation will declare war on another nation, the first thing it does is evacuate its ambassadors. Because Christians are ambassadors of Christ (2 Corinthians 5:20), it makes sense that God will airlift us off the earth and bring us safely to heaven before He declares war on the earth. In Revelation 3:10, Jesus promises that He will keep His church "from the hour of trial that is going to come upon the whole world."

Jesus points ahead to an unspecified future time of unprecedented universal, worldwide trouble, the final Day of the Lord, when God will judge all the unbelieving inhabitants of the earth. Revelation 3:10 doesn't say that Christians will be protected from God's wrath "during" the tribulation, nor guarded "through" the tribulation, but delivered "from" or "out of" the "hour of trial." Thus, the church will be removed from the earth before the time of this trial begins.

Ten: NO WRATH ON THE CHURCH. 1 Thessalonians 5:9 clearly states, "For God did not appoint us to suffer wrath but to receive salvation through our Lord Jesus Christ." Romans 5:9 echoes, "Since we have now been justified by his blood, how much more shall we be saved from God's wrath through him!"

Since the tribulational woes are universal in scope (Revelation 6:17), no one on earth will escape them. However, those who are part of the Bride of Christ, whose sins have been paid for fully by the blood of Christ, are exempt from ever suffering God's wrath (Romans 3:24-26; Colossians 2:13-14; Hebrews 10:14).

God rescued Noah from the Flood (Genesis 6-9), and rescued Lot before destroying Sodom (Genesis 18-19), showing that God does not pour out His wrath on believers. Therefore, logic dictates that the church will not be present on earth during the universal outpouring God's wrath.

But What About....?

One crucial passage used to argue against the pretribulation rapture is 2 Thessalonians 2:1-4:

> Concerning the coming of our Lord Jesus Christ and our being gathered to him [the rapture], we ask you, brothers, not to become easily unsettled or alarmed by some prophecy, report or letter supposed to have come from us, saying that the day of the Lord has already come. Don't let anyone deceive you in any way, for that day will not come until the rebellion occurs and the man of lawlessness is revealed, the man doomed to destruction. He will oppose and will exalt himself over everything that is called God or is worshiped, so that he sets himself up in God's temple, proclaiming himself to be God.

The Thessalonians were "scared out of their wits" with sweaty palms and white knuckles, fearing they had somehow missed the rapture and that the day of the Lord had arrived. Paul wrote this section in order to correct their misconceptions.

Apostasy and Antichrist

According to this passage, two events must precede the "day of the Lord" when God pours out His wrath during the Great Tribulation. First, the "rebellion" must occur. Second, the "man of lawlessness" must be revealed. The "rebellion" in Greek is *apostosia,* which means "apostasy," "departure," "falling away" or "total abandonment." Following the rapture of all true believers, all those who remain behind in the organized "Christian church" will be unbelievers only. Without any "conservatives" with biblical convictions to hold them back through the preaching of the gospel, unsaved churchgoers will quickly dive into deep doctrinal apostasy and completely abandon the true faith. The "man of lawlessness" refers to the future world ruler. The antichrist will be revealed when he establishes a seven-year covenant of peace with Israel. Three and a half years later, when he demands to be worshiped as god, his identity will be unmistakable.

So, the two events that precede the wrath of God in the day of the Lord are apostasy and antichrist. Many people assume Paul states that the rapture will not happen until after these two events have taken place, but he does not. All he states is that the "day of the Lord," the judgment portion of the tribulation, will not begin until after these two events occur.

What this implies is that there will be a gap of time between the rapture and the day of the Lord (which starts in the middle of the Daniel's seventieth week). This gap will extend for at least three and a half years. During this gap of time, after the church is gone, the apostasy will occur and the antichrist will arise.

The seven-year tribulation will not begin on the day of the rapture. The seventieth week of Daniel 9:27 begins only after the antichrist has gained sufficient power to enact and enforce a peace treaty with Israel. Since the antichrist won't be revealed while the church is present on earth, additional time is needed to allow for his rise to power. Therefore, the rapture will occur more than seven years prior to the second coming of Christ to the earth.

Who Holds Back Antichrist?

In 2 Thessalonians 2:6-7, Paul tells us that the antichrist is now being held under control by a powerful Person:

> And now you know who is holding him back [the restrainer], so that he [the antichrist] may be revealed at the proper time. For the secret power of lawlessness is already at work; but the one who holds it back will continue to do so until he is taken out of the way.

Who is holding back antichrist? In the Greek text, He is mentioned once with a neuter particle and once with a masculine pronoun. This fits only one Person, the Holy Spirit.[49] This change from neuter to masculine gender is an important, hidden clue to His identity. Galatians 5:17 and Romans 8:5-9 teach that the Holy Spirit's job is to counteract the effects of evil. Genesis 6:3 identifies the Holy Spirit as the One who restrains sin. Clearly, it is the Holy Spirit who holds back the antichrist at the present time. Only omnipotent God is powerful enough to restrain satanic evil.

Question: What actually happens when the Holy Spirit is "taken out of the way"?

Answer: Where does the Holy Spirit live on earth? He lives within the bodies of Christians. Believers' bodies are temples of the Holy Spirit. The universal church collectively functions as one temple in which the Holy Spirit dwells on earth. Therefore, when the church, the

---

[49]John 15:26; 16:6-7,13-14; Ephesians 1:14.

Holy Spirit's temple, is raptured from the earth, the Holy Spirit is also "taken out of the way."

As omnipresent God, the Holy Spirit will still be present everywhere on earth. He will actively bring people to salvation throughout the tribulation. His other ministries will continue just as they did in Old Testament times before the day of Pentecost. With the church removed, the Holy Spirit will be removed only in His role of holding back antichrist through His indwelling of Christians. His role of preserving society from decay and destruction through the salt and light of Christians in the culture will be over because the Church, which He indwells and fills, will be gone.[50]

After the Holy Spirit is "taken out of the way," 2 Thessalonians 2:8-12 adds:

And then the lawless one will be revealed, whom the Lord Jesus will overthrow with the breath of his mouth and destroy by the splendor of his coming. The coming of the lawless one will be in accordance with the work of Satan displayed in all kinds of counterfeit miracles, signs and wonders, and in every sort of evil that deceives those who are perishing. They perish because they refuse to love the truth and so be saved. For this reason God sends them a powerful delusion so that they will believe the lie and so that all will be condemned who have not believed the truth but have delighted in wickedness.

Once the rapture occurs, God's restraint of evil on the earth will be lifted. The church, through which the indwelling Holy Spirit now preserves the world through its influence of moral principles and gospel preaching, will be gone. Without the Church here to stop him, the antichrist will ascend to prominence within a short time. The false prophet, promoting a one-world religion that wows the world with satanic miracles, will champion his rise to

---

[50]For a more detailed analysis of this passage, see John F. Walvoord, "Escape from Planet Earth," in Foreshocks of the Antichrist, 374-78.

power.

People who have heard and rejected the gospel in these final days before the rapture will be deluded to swallow this deception hook, line and sinker. They will embrace the new "United Religions" that likely will combine apostate Christianity with Islam under a false Pope. In their spiritual blindness, they will worship the antichrist instead of the true God. This will lead to their condemnation under the holy judgment of God.

The final seven years of history before Christ's return to earth will not officially begin until the antichrist has gained sufficient power to enact and enforce a seven year peace treaty with Israel (Daniel 9:27). Once he signs a seven year covenant with Israel, guaranteeing her security from Islamic attack and permitting Israel to rebuild her temple in Jerusalem, the final seven year countdown will begin.

Many people discount the idea of a pretribulational rapture by arguing that no one taught this view until 1830. That's not true. In 373 A.D., Ephraem the Syrian, a major theologian in the early Byzantine Eastern Church, taught this:

> For all the saints and elect of God are gathered, prior to the tribulation that is to come, and are taken to the Lord lest they see the confusion that is to overwhelm the world because of our sins.[51]

This conclusively proves that at least some Christians believed in a pretribulational rapture even in the early days of church history.

It is reasonable to expect a pretribulational rapture. We must be fully ready each day for Christ to whisk us away in the twinkling of an eye (1 Corinthians 15:52) to meet Him in the air.

---

[51] Grant R. Jeffrey, *Final Warning* (Eugene, OR: Harvest House Publishers, 1996), 466.

Cosmic Cleansing?

How will it be explained when millions of Christians suddenly disappear and leave their clothing in a heap?

*As a mass abduction by aliens in UFOs?

*As a "cosmic cleansing" of mankind, surgically removing from earth "the cancer" who would interfere with mankind's next evolutionary quantum leap?

*As spontaneous chemical combustion of bodies sparked by nuclear stockpiles and toxic air pollution?

*As Mother Earth eliminating from Gaia's soul all who have a negative and narrow state of consciousness?

*As a deliberate purging of the population to save planet earth from ecological destruction?

We can't know for sure what the official explanation for these mass vanishings will be. But we do know that many who are left behind will surrender their freedom to a humanitarian savior in order to embrace his false offer of peace, prosperity and security.

Revelation, the 66th book of the Bible, is neither an impossible puzzle nor a playground for fanatics. You don't have to be scared to death to read its 404 verses. With the Holy Spirit as your Teacher and Guide, God can use this final prophecy to radically change your life.

Revelation teaches that beyond all the scenes of judgment, and beyond all the terrible descriptions of blood and slaughter and darkness and heartache and sorrow and misery, there is coming a new day, a wonderful day of victory and joy–a day when Jesus will win. The utopia that men have dreamed of for centuries will become a reality when Christ personally returns to the earth.

When Jesus Christ came to earth the first time, He was just a vulnerable baby. When He comes the second time, He will be an invincible warrior. The first time, only a few shepherds saw Him. The second time, every eye will see Him. The first time He came, a single star marked His arrival. The second time He comes, all the stars will fall from the sky, and He Himself will light the world.

Two thousand years ago, men made bold predictions about the future. These detailed, specific predictions are being fulfilled at an astonishing rate, with dazzling accuracy, right before our eyes. Skeptics used to scoff at the Scripture's nightmarish predictions of a globe exploding with catastrophes and tottering on the brink of extinction, but no one's laughing anymore. The idea of a fiery incineration engulfing the globe is, for the first time in history, a very serious threat.

God is now arranging the world stage for the final act of human history. When a benevolent messiah figure arrives to mesmerize the world, it will begin the most dramatic, deadly drama of all time. The world stage is still empty of specific actors, but the props are all in place, and the house lights are beginning to dim. The world is focused on a bull's-eye called Jerusalem. It is unmistakable. It is real. It is happening now. The rapture of the church is about to occur very, very soon.

What are you supposed to do about it? Should you go on wasting 30 hours a week in front of a TV set, complacently assuming it will never happen in your lifetime? Are you to pretend that these things are not really happening around you? Not on your life.

The Lord Jesus Christ expects you to watch, witness, worship, walk and work until He comes.

When you see the downtown merchants decorating for Christmas, you know that Thanksgiving is near. In the very same way, when you see the world stage being set for the tribulation, you know that the rapture must be near. It won't be long until "we're outa here!"

My personal summary of future prophetic events is pictured on the following chart:

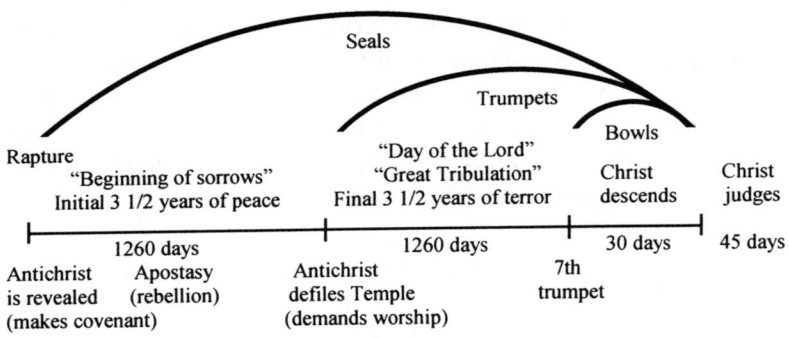

Overview of the Seven Year Tribulation

Appendix C

An Outline of <u>Revelation</u>

Text	Message Title
1:1-8	Christ Is Coming Back Soon
1:9-20	Christ Is In Charge Right Now
2:1-7	Christ Counsels His Church on Love
2:8-11	Christ Counsels His Church on Suffering
2:12-17	Christ Counsels His Church on Compromise
2:18-29	Christ Counsels His Church on Tolerance
3:1-6	Christ Counsels His Church on Apathy
3:7-13	Christ Counsels His Church on Embarrassment
3:14-22	Christ Counsels His Church on Complacency
4:1-11	Christ's Father Is Wholly Holy
5:1-14	Christ Is Our Worthy Lion and Lamb
6:1-17	Christ Opens Six Seals of Judgment
7:1-17	Christ Calls 144K To Save Millions
8:1-9:21	Christ Sends Six Trumpets of Doom
10:1-11:19	Christ's Two Witnesses of Warning
12:1-16	Christ's War with Satan the Serpent
13:1-18	Christ Permits Antichrist To Emerge
14:1-20	Christ Harvests Souls from the Earth
15:1-16:21	Christ's Final Wrath In Seven Bowls
17:1-18	Christ Kills the Scarlet Harlot
18:1-24	Christ Destroys Proud Babylon
19:1-10	Christ Reigns–Sing Hallelujah!
19:11-21	Christ Returns In Complete Victory
20:1-6	Christ Rules For 1000 Years of Peace
20:7-15	Christ Sends Satan to a Lake of Fire
21:1-22:6	Christ Creates a New Heaven and Earth
22:7-21	Christ Invites You to Come to Him

For sample sermon manuscripts, see the author's web site at http://UntilChristComes.com/Bible.html

Appendix D

Selected New Testament Index

To order more copies of "What To Do Until Christ Comes," please duplicate this page and send in the completed form!

Ship to (please print):

Name: _____

Address: _____

City/State/Zip:. _____

Day Phone: _____

Email: _____

I'd like to order _____ copies at $12.95 each ....$ _____

Shipping/postage is $3.50 (regardless of quantity)...$ _____

Add 7.6% tax (Washington residents only) ....$ _____

Canada (add $2.00); International (add $5.00).........$ _____

TOTAL AMOUNT ENCLOSED...........................$ _____

Make your check of money order payable to Dale Johnsen

Mail it with the above shipping information to:
Dale Johnsen
11502 Sara Loop
Yakima, WA 98908-9253

(Please allow up to three weeks for shipping.)

You may direct inquiries about quantity ordering via email to:
johnsen@UntilChristComes.com
or Dale@Pastors.com

You may also direct friends and family to read sample chapters of this book on-line at no charge before ordering! Just ask them to point their web browser to **http://UntilChristComes.com/**

To order more copies of "What To Do Until Christ Comes,"
please tear out this page and send in the completed form!

Ship to (please print):
Name: _____
Address: _____
City/State/Zip:. _____
Day Phone: _____
Email: _____

I'd like to order _____ copies at $12.95 each ....$ _____
Shipping/postage is $3.50 (regardless of quantity)...$ _____
Add 7.6% tax (Washington residents only) ....$ _____
Canada (add $2.00); International (add $5.00) ....$ _____
TOTAL AMOUNT ENCLOSED ....$ _____

Make your check of money order payable to Dale Johnsen

Mail it with the above shipping information to:
  Dale Johnsen
  11502 Sara Loop
  Yakima, WA 98908-9253

(Please allow up to three weeks for shipping.)

You may direct inquiries about quantity ordering via email to:
  johnsen@UntilChristComes.com
  or Dale@Pastors.com

You may also direct friends and family to read sample chapters of
this book on-line at no charge before ordering! Just ask them to
point their web browser to **http://UntilChristComes.com/**

To order more copies of "What To Do Until Christ Comes,"
please tear out this page and send in the completed form!

Ship to (please print):
Name: _____
Address: _____
City/State/Zip:. _____
Day Phone: _____
Email: _____

I'd like to order _____ copies at $12.95 each ....$ _____
Shipping/postage is $3.50 (regardless of quantity)...$ _____
Add 7.6% tax (Washington residents only) ....$ _____
Canada (add $2.00); International (add $5.00) ....$ _____
TOTAL AMOUNT ENCLOSED ....$ _____

Make your check of money order payable to Dale Johnsen

Mail it with the above shipping information to:
    Dale Johnsen
    11502 Sara Loop
    Yakima, WA 98908-9253

(Please allow up to three weeks for shipping.)

You may direct inquiries about quantity ordering via email to:
    johnsen@UntilChristComes.com
    or Dale@Pastors.com

You may also direct friends and family to read sample chapters of
this book on-line at no charge before ordering! Just ask them to
point their web browser to **http://UntilChristComes.com/**

To order more copies of "What To Do Until Christ Comes,"
please tear out this page and send in the completed form!

Ship to (please print):
Name: _____
Address: _____
City/State/Zip:. _____
Day Phone: _____
Email: _____

I'd like to order _____ copies at $12.95 each ....$ _____
Shipping/postage is $3.50 (regardless of quantity)...$ _____
Add 7.6% tax (Washington residents only) ....$ _____
Canada (add $2.00); International (add $5.00) ....$ _____
TOTAL AMOUNT ENCLOSED ....$ _____

Make your check of money order payable to Dale Johnsen

Mail it with the above shipping information to:
    Dale Johnsen
    11502 Sara Loop
    Yakima, WA 98908-9253

(Please allow up to three weeks for shipping.)

You may direct inquiries about quantity ordering via email to:
    johnsen@UntilChristComes.com
    or Dale@Pastors.com

You may also direct friends and family to read sample chapters of
this book on-line at no charge before ordering! Just ask them to
point their web browser to **http://UntilChristComes.com/**